CROMBIE

THE WONDER BOOK
OF
DARING DEEDS

THE BLIZZARD.

PIPER FINDLATER (GORDON HIGHLANDERS) WINNING THE V.C. AT DARGAI.

[*Frontispiece.*

THE WONDER BOOK
OF
DARING DEEDS
TRUE STORIES OF HEROISM AND ADVENTURE

WITH
EIGHT COLOUR PLATES AND NUMEROUS ILLUSTRATIONS

General Editor: HARRY GOLDING, F.R.G.S.

WARD, LOCK & CO., LIMITED
LONDON AND MELBOURNE

MADE IN ENGLAND
Printed in Great Britain by
L. T. A. ROBINSON LIMITED, THE BOTOLPH PRINTING WORKS, LONDON

[*Fox Photos.*

Squadron Leader F. R. D. Swain testing and adjusting his high-altitude suit and apparatus.

COLOUR PLATES

A dog team in the Far North.

CONTENTS

CONTENTS

H.M.S. Lion under fire at the Battle of Jutland.

[Photopress.

IN THE ICE.

[Central Press.

Amundsen's tent in the Antarctic.

FROZEN TO DEATH

The Memorable Tragedy of Captain Scott.

ON the 16th of January, 1912, five men were hauling a heavy sledge across the white wilderness that forms the Antarctic plateau. Tanned by long exposure to wind and the glare from the snow, wearied and worn down by two and a half months' incessant activity in tramping, hauling, making and breaking camps, they were still borne up by the thought that in one day more, or at most two, they would stand at a Pole of the Earth, where never human foot had trod before. These men were Captain Scott and his companions, the last of a party of twelve who had ascended to that desolate region ; their comrades had been sent back and they alone were intended to reach the goal. Their story, parts of which are familiar to everyone, is an epic of the British nation ; but it is good for us to consider once more who were the men who did this thing, and how they played the game right through to the inevitable end.

They had now been marching for more than eight hundred miles, a distance which would span the gap between the Shetland Islands and Land's End. The first half of the route had been pioneered by Scott himself during his first famous expedition ten years before ; the second half had been pioneered by the equally persistent and courageous Shackleton only three years since, and even now the polar party was but a few miles beyond his farthest point. This route started from the winter quarters on Ross Island, where three successive Antarctic expeditions had stayed. Early that spring Scott and his many willing helpers had continued the task (already commenced in the preceding autumn) of laying down depôts along their course ; for in that part of the world there is neither bear nor musk-ox, seal nor fox, nor, indeed any life at all except a few microscopic plants : everything the explorers needed, from fuel to tents, had to be taken with them or stored in depots so that it could be drawn upon when most needed.

The contemplated journey was rather more than double that which Peary marched to the North Pole (page 99) ; and if it had the advantage that the men were not on moving floes, with a restless sea beneath, it also had disadvantages—much greater cold, gales of a ferocity not found elsewhere in the world, a great continent which

[*Central Press.*

Where the glacier joins the sea.

[*Wide World Photo.*

A big berg.

had to be climbed to two and a half times the height of Ben Nevis, and surfaces of snow so granular and sand-like that the sledges became literally " bogged " in them. For a distance equal to that between London and Edinburgh, Scott's parties had laid out depôts every sixty-five miles, besides which snow mounds were built at frequent intervals to point the way ; for the whole of this part of the journey crossed an immense ice plain near sea level, with a mountainous coast rising into gaunt though lovely mountains far away on the right hand and nothing whatever visible on the left. When the sky was overcast, as often happened, and everything looked one hopeless pall of grey, it was extraordinarily difficult to steer in any direction ; for the compass was almost useless so near to the Magnetic Pole and the few distant landmarks had vanished.

All these difficulties were surmounted, the various sledge parties arriving at last at the base of a huge white glacier that rose ahead through the mountains. Shackleton, who found it, had aptly called it " The Gateway to the South Pole " ; and up it Scott's people had to march, whatever the difficulties, so as to reach the ice plateau on which the Pole itself lies. For many miles they had to climb among dangerous clefts into which men often slipped, and in the teeth of violent head-winds that brought blizzards of blinding, powdery snow down upon their heads ; and as the men struggled on, sweating with the extreme labour of pushing the sledges bodily through this sort of thing, sometimes they sank thigh-deep in the snow, sometimes fell right through a snow bridge into a bottomless crevasse, to be held up only at the last moment by a furious jerk of their hauling harness. Up to the base of the glacier most of the pulling had been done by dogs and ponies ; but now, at Shambles Camp, the ponies had all had to be shot, while the dogs had been sent home ; for Captain Scott, who hated cruelty to animals, could not endure the common polar practice of killing the dogs to feed each other ; and he preferred to manhaul his sledges by sheer strength and grit, a noble task even if it was an exhausting one. At last even the glacier's difficulties had been overcome ; the last of the supporting parties had been sent back ; the spot where Shackleton had unfurled Queen Alexandra's little silk flag had been attained ; and now, as we remarked at the outset, Scott and his four companions looked eagerly towards their goal. They were the more eager because a party of Norwegians, working from another part of the Antarctic, was also known to be in the field ; and for many reasons Scott desired to reach the Pole first.

[*Topical.*

Captain Scott looking for pack-ice.

At this moment, Bowers' sharp eyes detected a black spot far across the ice. With rapidly growing fears they hastened towards it, to find that they had been forestalled ; for it was a black flag tied to a sledge runner, and all around were the footprints of dogs and the signs of a camp. These things meant that

[Photopress.

Lieutenant (now Admiral) Evans with the instrument used to fix the position of the South Pole.

Amundsen and his men had stolen the crown which Scott, after all his toil and effort, had hoped to grasp; they had in fact reached the Pole just a month before, and but for his repeated misfortunes Scott and his men might even have met them there. They had every right to go, mark you, for their route lay across a region which no soul had ever seen; but it was a bitter pill to the Englishmen. Yet Scott's first thought now, as ever, was for those with him: "I am very sorry for my loyal companions."

Next day they followed the track of Amundsen southwards, and on the 18th found his small tent, patched with brown leather, and with the Norwegian flag still proudly flying there; Dr. Wilson made a sketch of it which must be unique. Inside the tent were some supplies that Amundsen had thoughtfully left for Captain Scott, with a letter which he asked to be forwarded to King Haakon. These relics were carefully secured; and the Englishmen, having planted their own flag a little distance away, faced the ordeal of their long journey back. Scott, swallowing his discomfiture, wrote this day:

"Well, it is something to have got here. Now for the run home and a desperate struggle. I wonder if we can do it." Everybody knows the answer.

What manner of men were these, who thus determinedly set out to walk eight hundred miles, with patched sledges, worn footgear, and that fatal sense of failure which would creep in, despite the utmost optimism? Take the leader first.

Scott was forty-three years old, and though not abnormally big or strong, was undoubtedly the toughest man in his ship's whole company; he had proved this repeatedly, both recently and during the memorable marches of the *Discovery's* people, and he was to prove it again before his death. Patient, indomitable of will, tenacious of discipline, and even stern when necessary, he was a fine type of naval officer, who had endeared himself to a very miscellaneous crowd of fellow explorers. He was a wonderful organiser. He was, too, deeply interested in the scientific side of his expedition and would take any amount of pains to master its details; and on the other hand, he would as readily spend a morning playing football or in consulting with Oates about the ponies' head-cloths; or even (when his turn came) going through the ordeal of cooking the daily meal upon which his exhausted sledge parties revived their drooping spirits.

Nearly lost. One of the sledges breaks through a snow bridge.

The Polar Sea.

But above all, his very presence was an inspiration. Where Captain Scott was there could be few shirkers ; he who can say : " I was with Captain Scott in the Antarctic," has his character ready made without farther questioning. So much for the leader.

His chief of staff, Dr. Edward A. Wilson, was a Cheltenham man, tall, thin, of imperturbable good humour, deeply interested in bird life, and possessing a highly artistic pencil. As hard as the proverbial nails, " Uncle Bill " was the good genius of the expedition, just as he had been a main prop of the first. He had been known to walk for an entire day beside a sledge, quite sightless from the agonizing pain of snow blindness ; and yet the instant his eyes had regained some vision, out had come pencil and paper again, so that he might continue to sketch the coast as they marched. Only a few months before, he and Cherry Garrard had gone out in the depths of an awful Antarctic winter, for the sole purpose of observing the breeding habits of Emperor penguins ; this trip, which nearly cost both their lives, Garrard afterwards described as " The Worst Journey on Record." Wilson was the sort of man with whom one goes tiger-shooting : dependable in all and every circumstance.

Then there was the Cornish officer, Captain L. E. G. Oates, " Titus Oates " or " The Soldier " to his comrades, the gallant English gentleman, who gave his life for his friends. His job was the ponies, while they lived, and right well he did it. Since their deaths he had marched and pulled with the best.

Fourth was Lieutenant Bowers, of the Indian Marines, a short but extraordinarily wiry man, absolutely tireless, as Scott testified repeatedly, and a pillar of strength, ready for any kind of work. His prominent nose had caused him to be dubbed "Birdie Bowers"; and he was a general favourite, and was only at the Pole because Scott had taken him out of the last supporting party to reinforce his own strength. Bowers took most of the sights for position, a difficult and eye-aching task, but of course essential. At other times he pulled, strenuously, trying to assimilate his own short strides with the longer steps of his tall companions.

Last in this heroic band came P. O. Edgar Evans, "the strongest man in the ship." Evans had accompanied Scott on the latter's two

[*Topical.*

A sleigh party on the ice.

longest and most dangerous journeys, a fact which speaks for itself. Every detail of the sledges and their equipment came within his province; and only a few days before, Scott had been silently applauding his worth. His huge strength, too, was of the greatest assistance in the endless pulling of the laden sledges. Evans it was who, on being precipitated down a crevasse during the *Discovery* expedition, had to hang helplessly in space until Scott could haul him up; and then all he said was: "Well, I'm blowed!"

They turned back as soon as possible, so as to make a short march homewards on January the 18th. In places their outward track now proved a useful guide, but it was as often drifted over by fine snow. At times, too, they sailed the sledge along gaily with a following wind, Oates and Wilson in front, while Bowers hung on to guide it from behind; but for the most part each march was a sheer hard grind across the wind-blown snow ridges. Where these ridges were bad, the snow persisted in sticking to the runners and to the men's

CAPTAIN SCOTT AND HIS PARTY HAULING THEIR SLEDGE.

skis; six or seven miles was then reckoned a good march. This, unhappily, was far too slow; for summer was running away fast, and winter out there was unthinkable. Supplies of food began to run down, too; but on the 25th of January, when matters had become serious, they picked up a depôt.

Scott's diary, while not pessimistic, now records one misfortune after another. First Wilson strained a leg, and for an entire day could not pull; hobbling quietly along by the sledge to ease the inflamed limb. Oates began to acquire suspiciously cold feet; and Evans, who had badly cut his hands during the journey out, now got them severely blistered; his nose was also repeatedly frost-bitten—certain signs that his constitution was not standing the strain. Yet there could be no rest from the daily grind, except such as a blizzard supplied when it confined them to the tent; their needs were too great and urgent to brook delay. At length land came in sight, the first bit of rock which had been seen for seven weeks; and they began the dangerous descent of the glacier.

Disasters now followed one after another. They became involved in a maze of crevasses, and both Scott and Evans fell in; the latter now had slight concussion to add to his other ills. Twice the crevasses became so numerous and dangerous that Scott altered the course so as to clear them; yet each time the little band got into a worse maze than before, with no means of crossing the abysses except by the feeble snow bridges. At these places they took off their skis, which is curiously unlike the practice of Amundsen's people, who in similar circumstances relied upon the long skis exclusively. Scott's men had many a thrill, unasked and unwanted, "falling into crevasses every minute—most luckily with no bad accidents." The second time that this happened they had to camp amid the chaos of ice pillars and mountain mists (12th February), with food only for one meal left; nevertheless Wilson, despite bouts of snow blindness, lost no opportunity of sketching the walls of the glacier. To crown everything, on the 17th, Evans, despite repeated protests from him that he was quite all right, fell behind and could pull no longer; and eventually he broke down altogether. Scott, going back, picked him up, only for the dying man to collapse in his arms; he had never really recovered from the concussion, and that night he died.

Poor Evans was buried at the foot of the glacier. The survivors, thoughtful and silent, then went on, out on to the ice plain, only to find its snow like desert sand ; so that they ploughed great tracks through it and oftentimes could scarcely move the sledge. But a depôt had yielded food again ; they fed on " pemmican and horse flesh, the best hoosh we ever had on a sledge journey " ; and if only the fuel had been more abundant, there might have been some hope. But somehow the oil supply was short ; this was a source of great anxiety to men who had to march in the teeth of strong winds, with fifty or sixty degrees of frost to whet their edge. The boots of the party got so hard that it often took an hour or more before they could be put on ; and soon there arose still more unhappy causes of delay, for Oates' feet, which had become frost-bitten, grew steadily worse. After a while he could not pull the sledge at all and was compelled to hobble slowly beside it ; this threw more work on the others, who were already strained to breaking point, besides reducing their speed ; for never would they march away from their disabled comrade. Scott, seeing how desperate the position had become, wrote in his diary : " God help us, we can't keep up this pulling. Among ourselves we are unendingly cheerful, but what each man feels in his heart I can only guess." He did *not* say that thirty pounds of the weight was fossils, of extreme scientific interest, which all were determined to carry through to the ship. Oates now became worse ; until it became evident to all, himself included, that this was his last march ; yet he did not complain, although he must have suffered agonies. When he realised how his own slowness was imperilling the lives of the other three, he asked to be left behind in his sleeping bag, but they refused to abandon him. " Poor chap," wrote the leader, " it is too pathetic to watch him ; one cannot but try to cheer him up."

The marches now became seven miles a day, six miles, even less. A depôt containing a ton of stores lay only forty-two miles ahead ; but they were now so enfeebled that Scott had to calculate a week as the probable time which would elapse before they reached it. They were, in fact, almost at the end of their tether. At last, on the morning of the 17th of March, Oates looked out of the tent and found a blizzard raging. He said to the others : " I am just going outside and may be some time." They knew what this meant and tried to dissuade him ; but he stumbled away and was never seen again. He had given his life that theirs might be in peril no longer. They left at this place a little cross, bearing the inscription : " Hereabouts died a very gallant gentleman " ; and struggled on towards One-Ton Depôt.

The next day, when they still had twenty-one miles to go, they battled against a fierce head wind in fifty-nine degrees of frost. "No human being could face it," declared Scott, who had now, unluckily, developed frostbite on the right foot. But desperate though the position might be, they still had a little oil in reserve and half a can in the stove; and they refused to despair. By the 19th, they were within eleven miles of the depôt, with its stores beyond value in their eyes; and this night fortune dealt them the final blow. A blizzard sprang up, which continued without intermission until they died. On the 21st it was decided that Wilson and Bowers should make a

[*Photopress.*

The late Captain Scott's ill-fated party.

desperate effort to reach the depôt; but if they ever started, the storm drove them back again immediately. Then came the unforgettable last words of Scott's diary. "We shall stick it out to the end, but we are getting weaker, of course, and the end cannot be far. It seems a pity, but I do not think I can write more.—R. SCOTT.—For God's sake look after our people." Thus to the very last his thoughts were for others, those in the hut and on the ship who looked to him for their salaries and rewards.

During those last dark hours, too, when death sat at his side, he wrote a long and very noble string of letters, in a firm and steady hand. There were messages of sympathy to Mrs. Wilson and Mrs. Bowers. To the latter he said: "I write when we are very near the end of our journey, and I am finishing it in company with two gallant, noble gentlemen. One of these is your son." To his friend Sir James Barrie: "I may not have proved a great explorer, but we have done the greatest march ever made." To Sir Edgar Speyer, who had largely financed the expedition, he wrote: "I thank you a thousand times for your help and support, and for all your kindness . . . If this diary is found, it will show how we stuck by dying companions and fought the thing out to the end." To his family: "Take comfort in that I die at peace with the world and myself—not afraid."

A relief party had actually been waiting at One-Ton camp for a week, and had turned back only a few days before. Throughout the winter the fate of the explorers remained unknown; but next spring a search party found them there, lying in the tent just as they had died—Wilson and Bowers as if asleep in their bags, and Scott with his arm flung across Wilson. There they lie now, in the eternal silence of the great white wilderness, with the gales for their watch-dogs and the whirling drift-snow for their shroud. For them Adventure was over. For us who knew or who have read of them, it will always remain.

B. WEBSTER SMITH.

[*Central Press.*

Fast in the ice.

PIPER FINDLATER, V.C.

FOR many years, and even up to the present time, the Khyber Pass on the North-west Frontier of India has been a constant source of trouble to the Government of India and Great Britain. The Pass itself is the only possible way between the North-west of India and Afghanistan in the wild and rugged mountains of that district. The equally wild tribesmen of Afghanistan, who are continually being incited to rebellion, seem to be unable to stop raiding the North-west Province of India and their raids have been the cause of the disquiet.

In 1881 the Government of India came to an arrangement with the Afridi tribesmen to safeguard the Khyber Pass. The main clause of this Treaty was the payment of a subsidy to the Afridis and, in addition, the Indian Government raised a regiment of local Afridis, trained them and gained their loyalty. These troops were stationed at vital points in the famous Pass to act as guards. For sixteen years there was comparative peace.

Early in October 1897 the Afridi tribesmen rose, forgetting the benefits they were getting from the Indian Government, and between forty thousand and fifty thousand tribesmen swarmed down on the Afridi guards in the Pass and wiped them out. Next they attacked the forts on the Samana range of hills near Peshawar.

The forts held up the raiders and news soon reached the Government. Within a few days General Sir William Lockhart, commanding the Punjab Army of 34,882 men, advanced against the Afridis, making the frontier fort at Kohat his base for the campaign.

This force advanced swiftly and on the 18th of October, 1897, with very little resistance captured the Dargai Heights. The Dargai Heights consist of a spur on the Samana Range, which flanks the Kurram Valley north of Thal, Shinawari and Hangu, and they are clearly visible from near Fort Gulistan. These heights are in a position that commands the surrounding country and, from a military point of view, very important.

Before long General Lockhart's troops were forced to abandon Dargai owing to a shortage of water and they retired some distance. At once, as might be expected, the Afridis moved up and reoccupied the heights.

Observers from near Fort Gulistan kept the position in view and, on the 20th of October, 1897, saw that the tribesmen were assembling in large numbers and building up "Sangars," or heavy breastworks of stones, and generally fortifying the heights.

At once the British troops moved up and attacked. Major-General Yeatman-Briggs, who was in command of these operations, ordered a frontal attack without delay, making no plan of tactics. Possibly he underrated the enemy, or thought the advance of the large British force would cause the Afridis to beat a hasty retreat. In any case, he neglected to make use of the twenty-four guns at his disposal and concentrate their fire on the defences. The tribesmen were not intimidated by the advancing troops, but met them with a hail of fire that halted them with heavy casualties and caused them to retire. It was an overwhelming situation, but the British soldiers went back in good order. Nevertheless, the fact that they had been forced to retire was a bitter blow and the Afridis gained heart as they saw the men retreat.

General Yeatman-Briggs immediately made plans for a second attack. It would be impossible to allow the tribesmen time to think over and celebrate a repulse of British soldiers. This time he ordered his artillery to concentrate their fire on the Afridi defences for three minutes, but he still adhered to a frontal attack. He then instructed the Gordon Highlanders and the 3rd Sikh Regiment to carry the heights.

Directly the guns ceased firing—creeping barrages had not been invented in those days and, furthermore, the guns themselves were not sufficiently reliable for such an evolution—the two regiments left their cover and began to advance over the rough and broken ground.

The troops had to cover a wide expanse before coming to grips with the enemy who, notwithstanding that they were considerably shaken by the artillery bombardment, greeted them with a hail of bullets. The Gordon Highlanders were subjected to the brunt of the rifle fire and for a few seconds the lines wavered as they encountered the stream of lead. It was not easy ground to move over at the best of times. They had to struggle up hill, faced by a foe that shot at them steadily and murderously from behind the shelter of their now battered sangars and rocks.

It was then that Piper George Findlater took a hand. Seeing his comrades waver, he sprang to the front with his pipes and began to play the Regimental March—the *Cock o' the North*—in an endeavour to urge the Gordons on. The men started to press forward again, when Piper Findlater fell, shot through both ankles. Once more there was dismay as the drone of the pipes stopped and the instrument dropped to the ground.

But Findlater was made of stern stuff. It was inconceivable to him that the Gordon Highlanders should be held up by a band of "niggers," as he called the tribesmen, however numerous. Forgetful of his own pain, he tried to get to his feet, but failed. Instead of giving up, he recovered his pipes from the battle-scarred ground and, finding them still intact, dragged himself to a rock. Hauling himself up, he sat erect and played the March, oblivious of the bullets that spattered thickly round him.

Inciting the tribesmen to rebellion.

His action was enough. Cheered by his example and inspired by the strains of the Regimental March, the Gordon Highlanders charged forward, forgetting the hail of lead in the excitement. For their part, the 3rd Sikhs swiftly followed the Gordon's lead and soon the two regiments were driving the wild and fearless Afridis from the Dargai Heights, this time for good.

That day 37 officers and men were killed and 156 wounded. It

Piper Findlater, though shot through both ankles, playing the Regimental March T

the North, and so inspiring the Gordon Highlanders to capture the Dargai Heights.

is stated that these casualties would have been considerably lightened if the guns had been used for the first attack, but it was undoubtedly due to Piper Findlater's heroic act that the position was eventually captured.

The war dragged on through the bitter winter, the troops suffering intensely from the severe cold. Frost and ice continually hampered their movements—it must be remembered that they had come from the heat of the lower parts of India—but on the 4th of April, 1898, peace was concluded, the Afridis paying heavy fines and surrendering numbers of rifles after being threatened with a new punative expedition in the Spring.

At the end of the action at Dargai, Piper George Findlater had been picked up and, after a painful and laborious journey by camel—the only possible transport for the wounded over the roughground—was taken to England. Soon after arriving at the famous Military Hospital at Netley in Hampshire, Piper Findlater was decorated with the V.C. by Her Majesty Queen Victoria.

The British troops moved up and attacked.

Lawrence loved these wild Arabs.

LAWRENCE OF ARABIA

IT seems probable that the greatest mystery man of the War may prove to be that strange cipher who will go down to history as *Lawrence of Arabia.*

Who was this man ?

Colonel T. E. Lawrence, to give him his full military title, though he was never a soldier in the real sense of the word, was, until 1913, a young Oxford student. He was of mixed Irish and Scottish descent. And he was a keen Arabic scholar with a flair for archæology. If the Great War had never happened, in all probability, Lawrence would have spent his life digging up the ruins of ancient cities, temples and tombs in Mesopotamia, Arabia, Egypt and elsewhere. Then he would have written books telling the world fresh truths about the ancient civilizations.

In 1910, when he was still a student of twenty-two, the magic and mystery of the East had already claimed him. The story of the old Crusaders had gripped him. And he set off upon his journeying. On foot he wandered through Palestine and Syria. He went to study the Saracen architecture, and to dig amongst the ruins. He became very friendly with the Syrian Arabs, the desert sheiks, and nomadic tribes. He almost forgot he was a Briton. He loved these wild Arabs so. He quickly picked up their dialects, lived their wild, free, open life, rode their camels and horses, and wore Arab clothes.

Absolutely fearless, speaking Arabic, wearing the long, white robes and embroidered headgear of the natives, his face tanned by desert suns, Lawrence was frequently mistaken for an Arab, even by the Turkish officials who then held sway over Syria, Palestine and Mesopotamia.

Back he came to Oxford to finish his studies. But the East had already claimed this strange mystery man. And when he had graduated at the University with honours, off he went east again, this time exploring the region of the Euphrates.

Then came the Great War.

Thomas Edward Lawrence was twenty-five now, and happened to be back in England for a brief holiday. He tried to join the Army. He was refused twice. The standard of physique was high at the outbreak of war, and Lawrence was a little man.

" You're not tall enough," he was told at the recruiting office. It has also been said that the Army doctors thought him a weakling ! Queer, wasn't it ? The previous year he had defied the whole Turkish garrison at Akaba on the Red Sea, in carrying out a little adventure of his own.

" I want to examine the ancient ruins on the Island of Faroun, Kommandant," was his request.

" It is forbidden," replied the Turkish Kommandant.

The island was in shark-infested seas a quarter of a mile off the mainland. But the Turks had refused for military reasons. They suspected Lawrence of being a spy.

There was only one boat on the beach, and the Turks removed it so that this stranger could not by any chance reach the island. The Turks didn't know Lawrence yet. They were to know him well enough later. This intrepid Englishman, knowing that when the heat became intense at midday, the Turks would take their siesta, waited his opportunity.

When the Turks were asleep, Lawrence quickly made a temporary raft out of little copper tanks used for watering the camels. Then he paddled off, reached the island, carried out his inspection of the ruins, and set off shoreward. That return journey very nearly ended the career of the brilliant young Oxford scholar. Wind and tide were against him. And the sharks, real man-eaters, began nosing his frail, ramshackle raft. He escaped almost by a miracle. This was the intrepid youth the British recruiting officers turned down twice at the outbreak of the Great War.

[*Wide World Photos.*

Colonel T. E. Lawrence in Arab dress.

Four months later, after the escape of the German warships *Goeben* and *Breslau* into Turkish waters, came the evil tidings for Britain that Turkey had allied herself with Germany and Austria and had declared war on Great Britain and France. And one morning, the news placards in Fleet Street announced:

"*Turkish army attacks Egypt! Suez Canal threatened!*"

It was no longer an European conflict. It had become a world war.

Germany's intentions had become unmasked. With the aid of the Turks she had resolved to declare a *Holy War* throughout the Mohammedan world, and set the East ablaze against Britain. The Suez Canal was one of the life lines of the British Empire.

"If we capture the Canal," declared the German High Command, "we sever Australia, New Zealand, South Africa and India from London —the boasted heart of the British Empire."

This attempt very nearly succeeded. So did the Holy War. If any one man can be said to have prevented it, that man was Lawrence.

How did it happen?

It was known, of course, even before the War, that hundreds of the wild Arab tribes throughout Arabia, Syria, Palestine and Mesopotamia hated their Turkish overlords, and had already made several unsuccessful attempts to regain their national liberty. Hitherto, however, the Turkish Army had been too powerful. And where small revolts had taken place, brutal massacres of Arab men, women and children had been carried out by the Turks.

This was the Arab opportunity to throw off the Turkish yoke. But there was no fiery, white-robed prophet who could unite the tribes and rouse them. The sheiks were too jealous of each other. Moreover, the Turks had strong garrison forces throughout all the Arab provinces. And failure meant more Turkish massacres.

There was one brave Arab Chief, however, Hussein, the Sherif of Mecca, who so far withstood the Turks as to refuse to declare a Holy War amongst his people. He had four resolute sons, one of whom was called Feisal. This family, revered throughout the Moslem world as the descendants of the Prophet, became a rallying point against the Turk.

The Turkish vengeance was swift. Even while a conference went on at Medina between the Turk and Arab leaders, in one of the suburbs of the holy city the Turkish soldiers began a fearful massacre. As usual, men, women and children were butchered in their houses. Those who were not butchered were burnt alive. This massacre caused a thrill of horror throughout Arabia. And the wild desert tribes, when they heard of it, instantly clamoured for vengeance.

But who was to lead the great Arab revolt? No great leader with calm, organising ability had yet arisen. Moreover, the Arabs still fought with muzzle-loading guns, spears and swords. The Turks, trained and armed by the Germans, had machine-guns, modern rifles, and artillery.

It was into this breach that Lawrence, the youthful Arabic scholar, quietly stepped. First he was sent by Lord Kitchener to Egypt. His knowledge of the Arabs, their language and their country, made him indispensable. But Lawrence was no soldier—of the

"TIDINGS OF THIS NEW PROPHET SPREAD ACROSS ARABIA."

traditional Army type—although he was a born leader. And while his maps of the Turkish provinces, his details of the garrisons, etc., were useful to the Intelligence Department, he soon fell foul of the Generals and the Cairo staff. "The young upstart!" they called him.

So they tried to get rid of him. This was just what Lawrence wanted. And by a stroke of good fortune, probably at his own request, he was sent to Arabia . . . apparently to see whether by any chance something could be done to unite the Arabs against the Turks.

At last Lawrence had found his real job. Instantly he set to work. And in a few short months, the Arab revolt in the desert was no longer a stalemate. Here at last, dressed in a long white silken robe, riding a race camel, speaking their own language, and living their own life, was the new prophet for which the tribesmen had been waiting. Feisal, the son of Hussein, the Sherif of Mecca, became Lawrence's great friend and faithful ally.

Tidings of this new prophet spread across Arabia. On camels and horses from north, east and south, the Arab sheiks came riding in with their tribesmen to join the revolt. They came, they saw, these wild sons of the desert. And, immediately, they fell under the spell of this white-robed Englishman.

"Allah be praised!" they cried. "This man will break the Turkish yoke!" Their enthusiasm knew no bounds.

But it was arms they wanted—rifles and machine-guns like the Turk. Big cannon which could send bursting shells amongst their enemies. More still, they wanted aeroplanes . . . big white birds. The German machines had already been dropping bombs amongst the tribes. Lawrence, speaking in their own tongue, promised them all these things.

"The British fleet will bring food," he told them. It was already shelling the Turkish Red Sea ports. "It will also brings guns and powder!"

When the Arab chiefs sat in council with Lawrence and Feisal, the son of Hussein, they were more bewildered still. This Englishman not only spoke their dialects, but he knew Arabia, Syria and Mesopotamia better than they knew the provinces themselves. He kept his promises, too, though there was some delay in getting the cannon and aeroplanes. But one day two *Bristol Fighter* machines with a *D.H.*9 arrived at the camp, and the Arabs were as delighted as children.

LAWRENCE HIMSELF WAS ALWAYS IN THE HOTTEST FIGHT.

C

"OFF HE WENT EAST AGAIN."

[*Topical*.

Aircraftsman T. E. Shaw (Colonel Lawrence) in working kit.

A little later, Lawrence having got a message through to General Allenby, who was beginning his drive in Palestine, the Arabs had a bigger surprise still. A huge *Handley-Page* bearing the now well-known Allied markings loomed up over the desert, flying toward the camp. Thrilled, the Arabs watched it circle round, then saw it land. Galloping their mounts toward it, they gazed at it in amazement. It had brought a ton of petrol and oil, with spare parts and rations.

"It is the Father of all the aeroplanes," they cried. "The others were but foals beside it!" But, when almost daily now, the Arabs saw the *Bristol Fighters* go up to fight with every Turko-German machine which appeared, their certainty of final victory over the Turks became assured.

Meanwhile, Lawrence was organising his army. He understood the Arab thoroughly. No use to make him fight in the open plains or in massed formation. In small guerilla warfare, on the enemy's flank, or in his rear, or in mountain warfare, the Arab was unequalled. Lawrence organised a hundred such bands. And before the war had finished, his fierce bands were springing one surprise after another upon the Turko-Germans. From Akaba on the Red Sea to Azrak, and right away north to Jerusalem and Damascus in Syria, this wild guerilla warfare continued. And Lawrence himself was always in the hottest fight.

Destroying the railway, blowing up bridges, and cutting communications behind the enemy front, causing endless dislocation and havoc, was for Lawrence's Arabs a daily occurrence. With dynamite and gelignite Lawrence blew up seventy-nine bridges, many of them with his own hands. And some of them were strongly guarded at the time.

Lawrence's strategy was sound. He attacked the enemy so repeatedly, and on such a far-flung front, that the Turks had to stretch their lines almost to breaking point to deal with the guerilla bands. And as a consequence, with bridges destroyed, and communications broken, ammunition and food supplies often failed the Turks. Isolated garrisons were captured, and the number of Turkish, German and Austrian prisoners became very considerable. Meanwhile, after the fall of Jerusalem, with Allenby sweeping through Palestine, and the French cleaning up Syria, the big Turkish retreat became a rout.

Through all this long and bitter fight of the Arab revolt, although the wild tribesmen often quarrelled with each other, for there were innumerable age-long blood-feuds, Lawrence was loved and trusted probably more than any white man has ever been loved in Arabia before. Yet always to the simple Arab he was something of a mystery man, and a prophet. Here was a man with no axe to grind. When

[*Central Press.*

Aircraftsman T. E. Shaw (Colonel Lawrence) and his motor-bicycle.

he was offered field rank, then decorations by both the French and British, he refused them. He loved the Arabs, and he risked his life a hundred times to free them from the Turkish yoke, and restore to them the independence for which generations of Arabs had longed.

Victory came at last with the end of the Great War. After centuries of tyranny and overlordship, the Arabs were free again. The Turkish yoke was broken for ever. Feisal, the son of Hussein, who had fought so long side by side with Lawrence, was declared King of Irak.

Lawrence felt that his work was done and asked permission to return to England. It was reluctantly granted by General Allenby.

Then came the sad leave-taking. Until that moment Lawrence never knew how much he loved the Arabs. There were tears in the eyes of the fierce desert warriors when they knew that " *Aurance* "—the nearest they could get to pronouncing his name—was really saying farewell. It was a sorrowful parting. They crowded about Lawrence, begging him to come back soon.

Back in England the whole country paid tribute to his work. Oxford University offered him a Fellowship. The British Government appointed him Adviser on Arab Affairs. He soon resigned both offices. He also discarded every rank and decoration his services entitled him to. It is believed that he was indignant because the war pledges he had given to the Arabs had not been fully honoured. He was always the Arab's friend.

Lawrence's last years, however, were just as mysterious as those earlier days. He disappeared for a while, and strange legends and rumours spread concerning him. Then it was found that he had changed his name and had enlisted as a private in the Tank Corps. He was discovered. Then, under the name of *Shaw*, he obtained a transfer to the Royal Air Force.

His end was tragic. He was killed in a road accident. And when the identity of the dead man by the roadside became known, the whole nation felt a stab of grief at his untimely end. That was Lawrence of Arabia.

He was certainly one of the great mystery ciphers of the War. Throughout the Empire and the world he has become a *name*. But in Arabia, wherever the Bedouin pitches his rude tent, or spreads his prayer mat, the name of " Aurance " has already become a *legend*.

ROWLAND WALKER.

[Fox Photos.

Squadron Leader F. R. D. Swain in his high-altitude machine.

FLYING NINE MILES HIGH

Squadron Leader Swain Establishes a New World's High-Flying Record for Britain.

EARLY one morning in September, 1936, a great silver-and-black monoplane stood on the R.A.F. aerodrome at Farnborough, its engine "warming up" in readiness for flight. Nearby stood its pilot, surely the strangest-looking airman who ever flew. Clad in a heavy suit of white rubberised fabric that covered his body from feet to neck, he wore upon his head a glass-fronted metal helmet—and looked for all the world like some robot man, or a diver about to descend to the ocean bed.

In fact, it was the heights and not the depths that he was preparing to explore, for this strangely-clad airman was Squadron Leader F. R. D. Swain, the man chosen by the Royal Air Force for its attempt to fly to a greater height than man had ever reached before and so capture for Britain the world's altitude record for aeroplanes. The curious suit which he wore was an airtight "pressure suit," specially designed to enable the wearer to withstand the very low pressure at high altitudes. Hermetically-enclosed within this suit and fed with oxygen through one side of the helmet the pilot would be able to live and breathe at those great heights where, otherwise, the rarefied, oxygen-starved air would spell unconsciousness and death.

The aeroplane in which this ambitious flight was to be made well deserves examination, for it has been specially built for exploration of the stratosphere—that mysterious region of the upper air, miles above the surface of the Earth, where there are no clouds but a bitter, unearthly cold, where no rain ever falls, but where, so scientists believe, winds of tremendous strength rage through space with the regularity of ocean currents. A low-wing Bristol monoplane, the machine is the largest single-seater aeroplane ever built, the great single wing measuring no less than 60 feet from wing-tip to wing-tip. The engine is a specially supercharged Pegasus air-cooled radial and drives a four-bladed wooden airscrew. For the sake of lightness, the whole machine is built of wood, but even so, when fully loaded and carrying some 80 gallons of petrol, its total weight is little short of two and a half tons.

The pilot's seat is in a glass-enclosed cockpit, warmed by air from the oil-coolers in the wings. Confronting the pilot is a dashboard bearing a confusing array of instruments and gadgets, oil and temperature gauges, rev-counter, blind flying instruments, compass, oxygen and heating controls—all of which must be closely watched throughout the flight. Just outside the cockpit there is a small panel let into the side of the fuselage. It bears the ominous-sounding instruction beginning:

"To open cockpit and release pilot, break seal and pull ring"
—a precaution in case the oxygen-breathing apparatus should fail and the pilot be forced to land in a fainting condition. As a further safeguard the pilot himself carried, in a sheath sewn on to the arm of his pressure-suit, a sharp knife for use in case of emergency.

But no thought of danger or disaster was in Squadron Leader Swain's mind on that momentous morning as, his heavy suit finally adjusted and sealed, he clambered awkwardly into his tiny cockpit and pulled close the sliding glass covers. A careful test of his engine, a final glance round the array of instruments, a last salute to the small group of officers standing on the aerodrome to watch him, and he took-off. The time was then exactly 7.30 a.m.

It was a clear, bright morning and at first he climbed in wide

By courtesy of] [" *Flight.*"

Squadron Leader F. R. D. Swain alighting from his machine after his record-breaking flight.

circles until the aerodrome he had left was lost to view, an undistinguishable patch in the vast panorama spread out beneath him. Within half an hour his altimeter showed a height of 40,000 feet. He increased his supply of oxygen slightly and turned south-east to

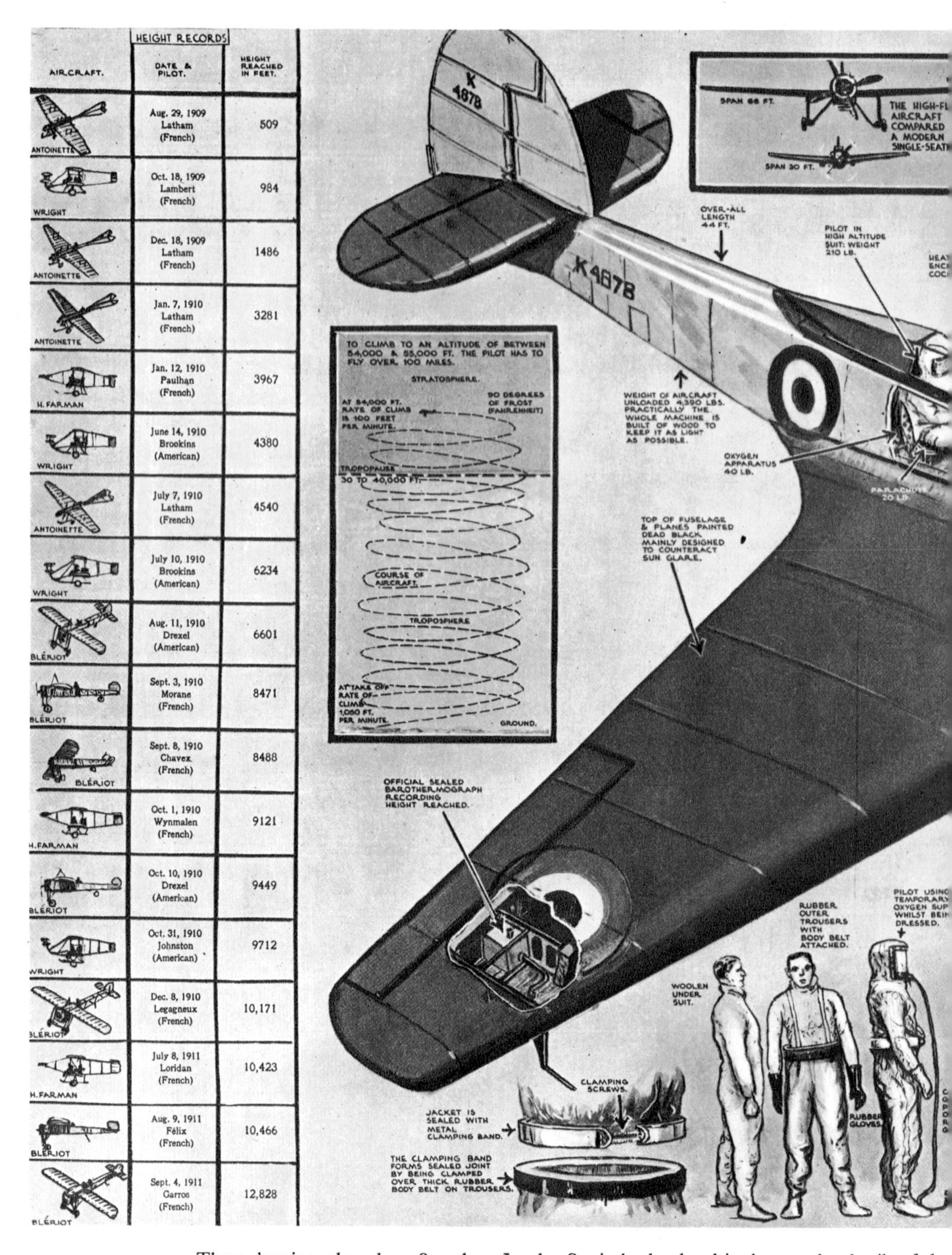

HEIGHT RECORDS

AIRCRAFT.	DATE & PILOT.	HEIGHT REACHED IN FEET.
ANTOINETTE	Aug. 29, 1909 Latham (French)	509
WRIGHT	Oct. 18, 1909 Lambert (French)	984
ANTOINETTE	Dec. 18, 1909 Latham (French)	1486
ANTOINETTE	Jan. 7, 1910 Latham (French)	3281
H. FARMAN	Jan. 12, 1910 Paulhan (French)	3967
WRIGHT	June 14, 1910 Brookins (American)	4380
ANTOINETTE	July 7, 1910 Latham (French)	4540
WRIGHT	July 10, 1910 Brookins (American)	6234
BLÉRIOT	Aug. 11, 1910 Drexel (American)	6601
BLÉRIOT	Sept. 3, 1910 Morane (French)	8471
BLÉRIOT	Sept. 8, 1910 Chavez (French)	8488
H. FARMAN	Oct. 1, 1910 Wynmalen (French)	9121
BLÉRIOT	Oct. 10, 1910 Drexel (American)	9449
WRIGHT	Oct. 31, 1910 Johnston (American)	9712
BLÉRIOT	Dec. 8, 1910 Legagneux (French)	10,171
H. FARMAN	July 8, 1911 Loridan (French)	10,423
BLÉRIOT	Aug. 9, 1911 Félix (French)	10,466
BLÉRIOT	Sept. 4, 1911 Garros (French)	12,828

These drawings show how Squadron Leader Swain broke the altitude record : details of the
At either side is a table of former record hol

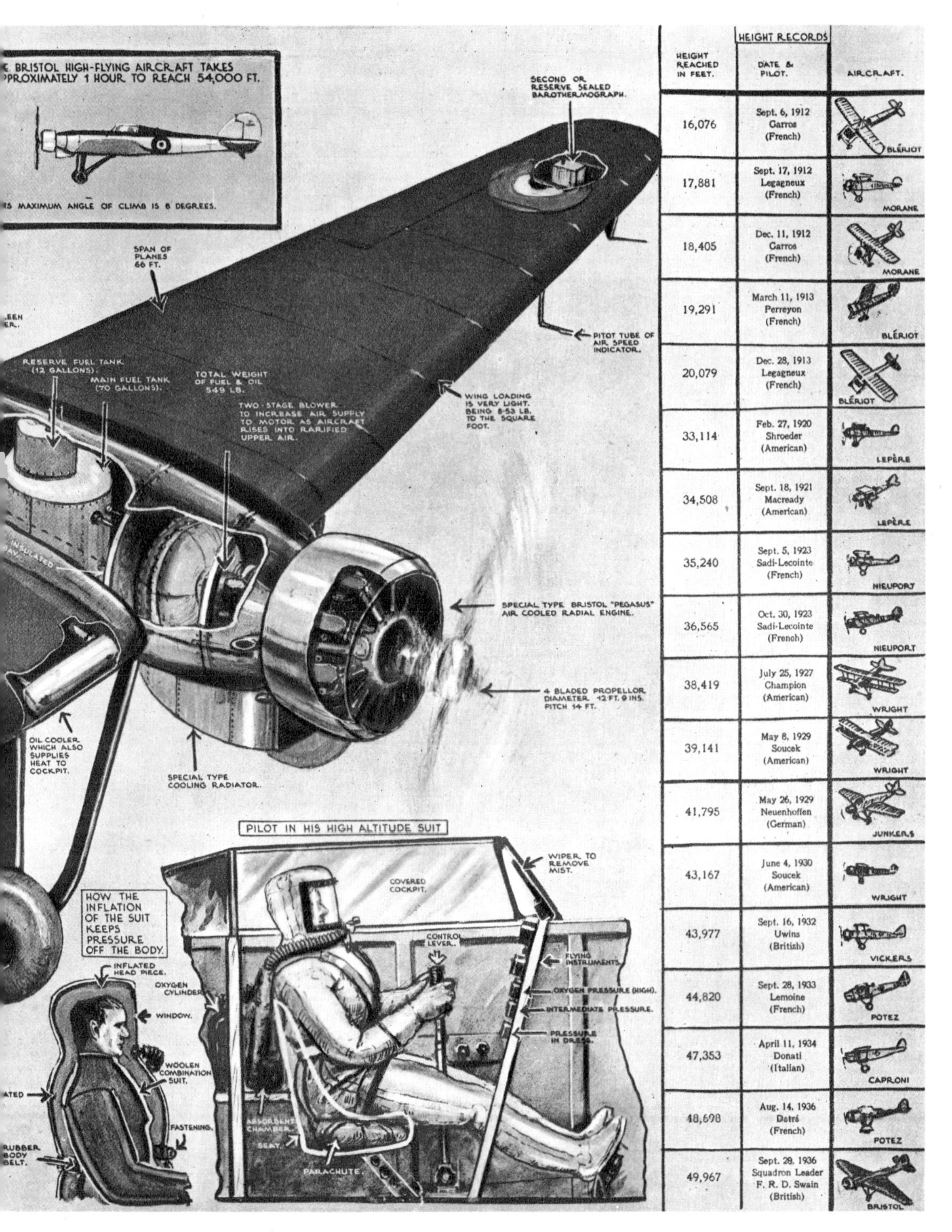

HEIGHT REACHED IN FEET.	DATE & PILOT.	AIRCRAFT.
16,076	Sept. 6, 1912 Garros (French)	BLÉRIOT
17,881	Sept. 17, 1912 Legagneux (French)	MORANE
18,405	Dec. 11, 1912 Garros (French)	MORANE
19,291	March 11, 1913 Perreyon (French)	BLÉRIOT
20,079	Dec. 28, 1913 Legagneux (French)	BLÉRIOT
33,114	Feb. 27, 1920 Shroeder (American)	LEPÈRE
34,508	Sept. 18, 1921 Macready (American)	LEPÈRE
35,240	Sept. 5, 1923 Sadi-Lecointe (French)	NIEUPORT
36,565	Oct. 30, 1923 Sadi-Lecointe (French)	NIEUPORT
38,419	July 25, 1927 Champion (American)	WRIGHT
39,141	May 8, 1929 Soucek (American)	WRIGHT
41,795	May 26, 1929 Neuenhoffen (German)	JUNKERS
43,167	June 4, 1930 Soucek (American)	WRIGHT
43,977	Sept. 16, 1932 Uwins (British)	VICKERS
44,820	Sept. 28, 1933 Lemoine (French)	POTEZ
47,353	April 11, 1934 Donati (Italian)	CAPRONI
48,698	Aug. 14, 1936 Detré (French)	POTEZ
49,967	Sept. 28, 1936 Squadron Leader F. R. D. Swain (British)	BRISTOL

" Aircraft, and the high-altitude pressure suit that enabled the pilot to live in the stratosphere.
the date of the feat and the altitude attained.

climb for another 5,000 feet. The cold and moderate wind that had been blowing at the lower levels had now become, at this great height, a gale of hurricane force and to avoid the risk of being blown out to sea Squadron Leader Swain turned into it and climbed on into wind.

In the pure, clear air at 46,000 feet the light was almost dazzling in its brilliance but, warned by his experience on previous trial flights, Squadron Leader Swain had had the upper surfaces of wings and fuselage painted black and was now able to look about him without being blinded by the reflected glare. The sky above him appeared as a very deep, almost indigo blue and no cloud had been seen since the 35,000 feet mark had been passed. He was now well into the stratosphere.

Forty-seven thousand feet above the South Coast, in the vicinity of Brighton, he peered down through the window of his helmet upon a map-like world below. So clear was the air that he could see the English coastline from Margate to Land's End and, northwards, to the Wash. London looked like a tiny toy town and the Thames was a narrow silver ribbon. Between England and the coast of France he could see the Channel Isles looking like pebbles in a river bed. To the lone airman, isolated miles above the Earth, and driving ever upwards through limitless space, there came a feeling of utter loneliness. It seemed impossible that that tiny country far below could be the England he knew, impossible that he could prevent himself from being blown far beyond its borders.

But there was work to be done and banishing the depression that comes upon even the bravest of airmen in the immense heights above the Earth, Squadron Leader Swain concentrated upon his instruments, watching compass, watch, oxygen indicator and altimeter as steadily he forced his machine ever higher. As he climbed and the difference in pressure between the inside of his suit and the outer air became steadily greater, the suit began to balloon outwards. This was an unexpected danger and as the swelling increased he found that it was becoming increasingly difficult to move his arms and legs, while a painful cramp had now developed in his right arm.

Still he kept on but the thin air at 50,000 feet was barely able to support the heavy 'plane and already the engine was starting to protest. Foot by foot he forced his way upwards, until at last his altimeter showed 51,000 feet and the labouring 'plane could be driven no higher.

One last look at the World spread out beneath him and he throttled back the engine and began the long glide back to Earth. He was then almost over the Bristol Channel and could see the Welsh mountains.

By courtesy of] [*The Bristol Aeroplane Co., Ltd.*

Squadron Leader F. R. D. Swain being assisted into his high-altitude pressure suit.

When he had dropped five thousand feet, he suddenly noticed that the windows of the cockpit were beginning to haze over. A few moments later the celluloid window of his helmet had also misted over. He could see neither instruments nor compass; all that he could make out was a distant glow that he knew to be the sun and, blindly, he turned towards it, knowing that by flying east he would at least keep above the land.

All the time the machine was steadily losing height, diving and rearing erratically, but kept in flying position by the superlative skill of a pilot trapped, blind and helpless, in his sealed pressure-suit. It was a perilous situation, and then, to make matters worse, Squadron Leader Swain felt a faintness stealing over him, as though he was being slowly suffocated. Fearing he was running short of oxygen, he tried to press the release lever which would open the cockpit cover, but found to his alarm that he had not the strength to move it. Then he tried to reach the ripping-panel on his suit, inserted for just such an emergency as this, but encumbered as he was by parachute and flying harness, he could not reach the rip-cord. Now blackness seemed about to engulf him and in desperation he grasped the knife on his arm, hacking and tearing at the celluloid window of his helmet.

At once the life-giving air blowing in through the rent revived him and, with the machine once more under full control, he discovered that he was now at 14,000 feet, over Somerset. He had plunged down for over 30,000 feet in his blinded and half-suffocating condition.

Still flying east, he continued to lose height until he reached Salisbury and, a few minutes later, he landed at the R.A.F. aerodrome at Netheravon with only two gallons of petrol remaining in his tanks.

Examination of the special height-recording instruments he carried showed, after making the necessary corrections for temperature and barometric pressure, that Squadron Leader Swain had penetrated into the stratosphere to a height of 49,967 feet—more than nine miles above the Earth—and had beaten the previous world's height record, set up by France, by the handsome margin of 1,270 feet.

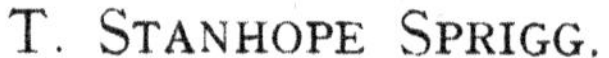
T. STANHOPE SPRIGG.

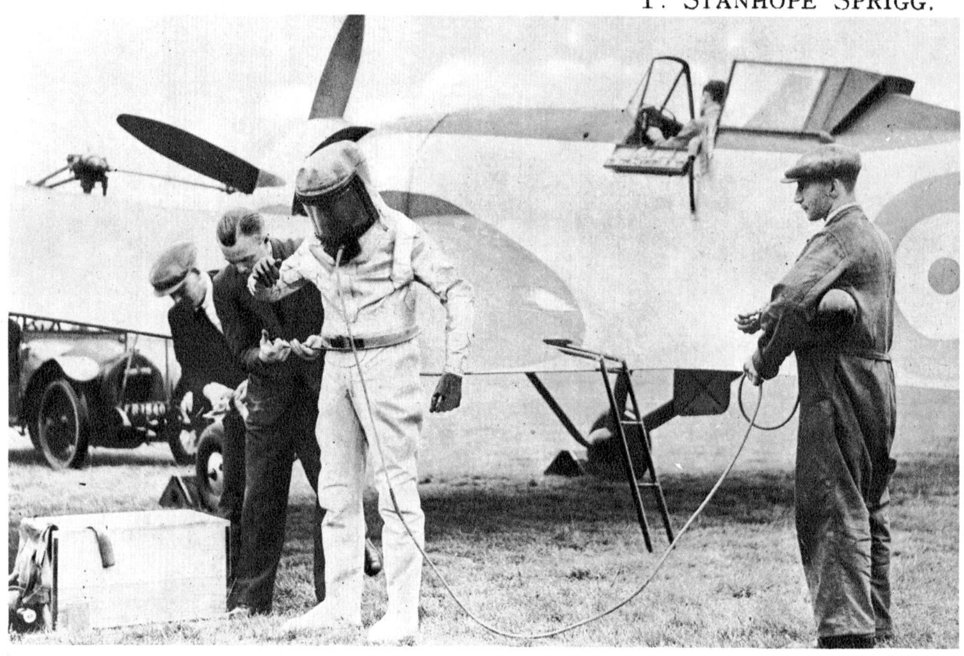

[Fox Photos.

Testing and adjusting his high-altitude suit.

[Wide World Photos.

The Bathysphere, with Dr. Beebe and Mr. Barton inside, being lowered into the depths of the ocean.

DOWN IN THE DEEP

How Beebe Sank Half a Mile in the Ocean.

MANY years ago Mr. H. G. Wells wrote a short story about a steel sphere, provided with portholes and padded cushions, in which the inventor sank through the ocean ; upon reaching the bottom, weights were released and he shot up again. People said that the tremendous pressure of the water would burst the windows and spread the inventor like butter over his own cushions ; but he came up alive, and he had extraordinary tales to tell of what he had seen. He then went down a second time and that was the last that was ever heard of him.

In 1930 a somewhat similar idea became a reality, thanks to the inventive skill of Mr. Otis Barton and the pluck and resourcefulness of Dr. William Beebe, the famous American naturalist. Beebe was no stranger to the sea-floor, having for years dived amongst the beautiful reefs off Bermuda ; he had even rubbed shoulders with sharks, and he regarded those sea wolves with a cool contempt. This latest adventure, however, was a vastly different matter ; for if you stand upon a plate that measures just twelve inches each way, then for every foot that you sink into the ocean sixty-four pounds is added to the load of water above you : at a mile down you would be carrying one hundred and fifty one *tons*, if you had not already been flattened out to a film. How then did Beebe and Barton contrive to sink half a mile (eight times as deep as a submarine can safely descend) and yet live to tell the tale ?

They used a Bathysphere, a hollow steel ball, four feet six inches in diameter. On one side it had a manhole through which a reasonably thin man might squeeze ; on the opposite side were three windows, two for observation purposes, but the third (which had originally been intended for a beam of electric light) was plugged with steel. The manhole was closed by a massive door and ten strong bolts ; the quartz windows were three inches thick. Inside the sphere there was just room enough for both men to wriggle about, and little besides ; after his first descent, Beebe carried the mark of a spanner on his anatomy for several days ! Air for eight hours was provided by cylinders of oxygen under great pressure, the gas being slowly released through a tap ; while the moisture and poisonous air exhaled by the two men were taken off by special chemicals in trays. When you add a cinecamera, a telephone, the electric light, and other impedimenta, you can understand the need for moving carefully within the Bathysphere ! The great ball, with its wooden stand, rested on the ship's deck ; and when in use was slowly lowered and raised from a stout drum by a non-twisting wire rope. Clipped to the rope at every hundred feet was a rubber telephone tube, by means of which Beebe from within the sphere gave orders or reported what he saw to the people on deck above, and even broadcast all over the world.

In this decidedly Wellsian contraption, Beebe and Barton ventured their lives off Nonsuch Island, Bermuda, on a calm June day in 1930. They wriggled through the manhole, the lid was shut, and they heard a tremendous din as the nuts were hammered home ; then, sealed up for good or ill, the Bathysphere was hoisted overboard and submerged. A slight splash, a sudden change from white light to green, a stream of air bubbles passing the windows, and Beebe saw the ship's bottom above him, draped with weeds and barnacles.

[*Wide World Photos (L.E.A.)*

Dr. William Beebe getting out of the Bathysphere.

The sphere sank so quietly that the motion passed unnoticed within, except that fish and shrimps seemed to swim upwards as they crossed the field of view. Outside the light changed from green to a rich and ever darker blue; although these colours were magnificent, there was not enough light for one to see even the lines of type on a printed page.

When they were three hundred feet down, Barton exclaimed, "Water's coming in!" and so it was, trickling slowly through the manhole rim; already a pint lay on the floor. Beebe instantly ordered the speed of descent to be increased ; and this, by forcing the sphere together with ever-growing pressure, fortunately stopped the leak. Thrilling though it was to hang down there in the middle of the sea, like a ball on a string, with a drop of more than a mile to the bottom if the string should break, both men were too busy to think of such things. Beebe in particular, his eyes rarely leaving the window, telephoned continuously everything that came into view ; and so excellent was the communication cord that he could distinctly hear the noises on the ship above. At one thousand four hundred and twenty-six feet—by which time it was bitterly cold in the water and the sphere had become chill and clammy—he had a feeling that they had descended far enough, so the order was given to haul in.

[*Wide World Photos.*

BABY DRAGONS OF THE OCEAN DEPTHS.

These young sabre-toothed viperfish, only about one inch in length, have enormous fangs with which they fight fiercely and seize their prey.

Meanwhile the brilliant yellow beam of the search-light had been shot out at frequent intervals, but not for long at a stretch because it heated and might crack the window ; whatever it picked up, especially if a fish, seemed afraid of the glare and swam off into the vague blue gloom beyond. Nothing sensational was seen—no huge sea serpents or other imaginary monsters; but many of the fishes were highly strange, such as the concertina-like Hatchet Fish, Lantern Fishes and so on; and in later descents they saw the hideous Angler Fish, with his huge open mouth, fringed with long, spiny teeth, ready to snap at any object that came too close to his waving tentacle. Then there were patches of softly-luminous jellyfish; deep-sea shrimps struck against the window and at once emitted a brilliant cloud of sparks;

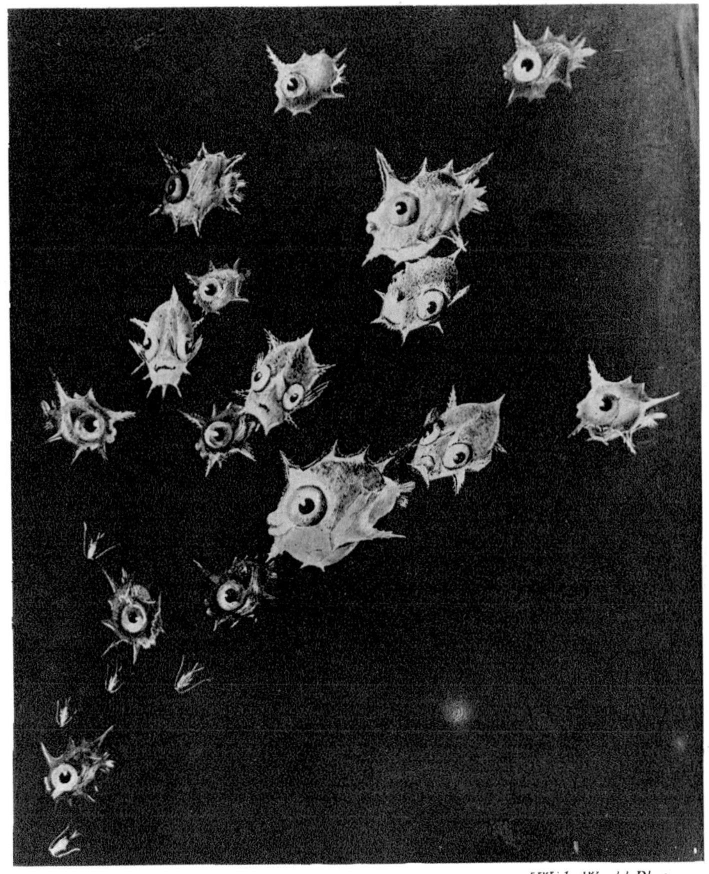

[*Wide World Photos.*

YOUNG OCEAN SUNFISH.

These little creatures grow from the size of a pin's head to monsters over a ton in weight.

and occasionally a shadow passed, as of some object several feet long, but too wary to come within the ray. Beyond the straight line of the light could be seen scores of tiny moving lights, which travelled hither and thither in the most bewildering way, like pale blue, green or yellow lanterns swaying in a garden at night—friends and enemies, feeders and food, and all strangely unreal to the observer peering at them from behind his window. These lights were the luminous spots of fishes and other animals, sometimes irregularly arranged, sometimes forming definite patterns, sometimes in rows like the portholes of an illuminated steamship. No human eye had ever seen them working naturally before.

Such was the memorable first descent of the Bathysphere. It

was followed by many others, during one of which (in 1934) Beebe and Barton reached a depth of three thousand and twenty-eight feet, more than half a mile. At this depth it was bitterly cold, both outside and inside the sphere ; and it was so dark that Beebe called it the blackest spot on Earth ; yet the lights of the hidden fishes, cuttle-fish, deep-sea shrimps, and so forth, were as numerous as ever. The pressure down there was so great that even the feeblest leak would have been fatal, as had already been shown by an extraordinary accident. The sphere had been sent down empty, with the bolts only partially tightened ; and when it came up it was three-parts full of water, while air under immense pressure was hissing out through a crack. To prevent accidents, the deck was cleared, and Beebe then began very gently and slowly to loosen the manhole lid ; when suddenly the pressure became irresistible, his hand was wrenched aside, and a bolt shot like a bullet through the air, severely denting the steel drum thirty feet away. Out of the Bathysphere shot a cloud of mist and water. Had the two scientists been within it when this accident occurred, they would have been crushed by mere air pressure.

B. WEBSTER SMITH.

[*Wide World Photos.*

"When the Bathysphere came up, it was three-parts full of water."

[Central News.

" The guns began to speak."

THE BOY V.C.

DAILY, from the 4th of August, 1914, to May, 1916, one question was repeated in every ship of the British Navy. It was a simple query, but the answer could not be expressed with any certainty. " When is Jerry coming out ? " was on the lips of every officer and man in the Senior Service, and the only reply was " today, perhaps."

Except for a brush off the Dogger Bank on the 24th of January, 1915, and two or three raids on the East coast, the German High Seas Fleet remained in the shelter of its harbours. U-boats and an occasional raider were the only enemy ships outside their own waters, while the British Fleet patrolled the North Sea and English Channel without ceasing.

On the 2nd of May, 1916, *H.M.S. Chester,* a Light Cruiser, was commissioned at Liverpool and proceeded to Scapa Flow to work up gunnery and other exercises with her new crew before joining up with the 3rd Light Cruiser Squadron. Amongst her crew was Boy (First Class) John Travers Cornwell, who was under sixteen years old.

H.M.S. Chester was kept busy after her arrival at Scapa Flow. On the 30th of May, 1916, she returned to her anchorage after carrying out an extensive Battle Practice and, to the joy of all on board, she was ordered to accompany the Fleet to sea the same evening. That was the first time she had sailed with the Fleet since her arrival at Scapa.

"Is the German Fleet out?" asked Jack Cornwell as they headed out to sea.

"Some hopes!" replied an A.B. "We're just going to steam up and down the North Sea for a bit and try to get Jerry to come out. We've done it every day, an' you can bet he won't come out when he knows *Chester* is waiting for him!"

"Anyway, we'll be ready for him if he does!" declared Cornwell. "Wait until we get the after port six inch trained on one of his ships!"

Jack was extremely proud of the fact that he was a member of that gun's crew. It was his duty to take orders from the after gun control and set the hands on the sight-setting dials as directed. It was no easy task in action, for although the telephone receivers were clamped to his ears in a tight-fitting helmet, the noise of gunfire made it necessary for him to be more than alert all the time.

Chester received orders to take up her position mid-way between the Third Battle Cruiser Squadron and the armoured cruiser screen which was in front of the fleet, to act as a connecting link for passing back signals to the Flagship.

Although it appeared that the ships were merely carrying out one of the routine 'sweeps' to the south-east, there was one factor that excited the few who were 'in the know'; the Battle Fleet was bringing up in the rear. As usual, rumours were flying about the lower deck. A wardroom messman had heard a few words spoken by one of the officers and had repeated them, in confidence, to his 'raggie.' These words, added to and suitably embellished, had been passed on from man to man, but still there were many that refused to believe—they had heard the messman's tales before.

By noon the following day it looked as if they were right. The ships were nearing the northern fringe of the Heligoland Bight, with its minefields, but there were no reports of German activity. An hour or so later the eastern limit of the sweep was reached and the signal to turn for home was made.

This turn was carried out by making a wide sweep round to the east. The weather was clear and visibility good. Towards 2.30 p.m. there was a buzz of excitement through the lower deck.

"Looks as if you'll have a chance of loosing off your gun at

Columns of spray rise in the water as enemy shells fall about the battleship.

Fritz, son!" remarked a seaman who had heard Cornwell's previous remarks. "They say the enemy has been sighted by *Galatea!*"

Cornwell was thrilled, but for some time there was nothing to substantiate the rumour. *Chester* was pelting ahead, but otherwise things were as usual from an official point of view until Jack Cornwell was on deck some time later. Seeing him, the Captain called him.

"Boy!" he ordered. "My compliments to the Engineer-Commander on watch. Tell him that if we wish to see any of the fun, it's time to hustle!"

Cornwell hurried away to the engine room and delivered the message.

All doubts were set at rest. There was to be a scrap!

At 5 p.m. 'Action Stations' was sounded. The crew rushed to their posts with even more alacrity than they had displayed at their practice and which had earned well-deserved praise only a few days before.

Jack Cornwell was well to the fore and almost before the notes of the bugle had died away he was strapping on his helmet with its 'tele-pads' at his gun.

Less than half an hour later the word went round that gun flashes were to be seen on the starboard bow. At that moment *Chester* altered course and increased speed to investigate. Excitement was at fever pitch. For his part, Cornwell could hardly realise that the shells stacked by his gun would be speeding at an enemy target in a few moments. His first big thrill came when he had to repeat orders from the After Control to 'load.'

Suddenly there was a mighty shout. Some light cruisers were seen on the port bow, rushing up through wisps of mist that were developing. At once a challenging signal was made: the reply was an immediate ripple of gunfire along the side of the leading light cruiser. There could be no mistake: Fritz was out and *H.M.S. Chester* was ready for him!

"Range seven thousand! Red forty!" The voice from the After Control sounded in Cornwell's ears. He set his dials to the figures—they indicated the range and direction in which the gun was to be trained.

Almost immediately the big guns began to speak.

He plainly heard the whine of the hostile shells as they tore overhead and, before orders came to fire the first salvo from *Chester*, the lad saw columns of spray rise in the water some five hundred to seven hundred yards from the ship's side. The enemy's second salvo had fallen short.

Almost at the same moment his own gun spoke, leaping back on its recoil and returning to its normal position like a live thing. Even as its crew jumped forward and opened the breech block to insert the new shell there was a sudden inferno of noise—the crash of shells on metal, then explosions and flying fragments of white-hot splinters and the searing scorch of the blast and reek of explosives.

In the midst of the noise of bursting projectiles, Jack Cornwell felt a violent, numbing shock that nearly threw him to the deck, followed by a tearing pain just below his heart. He clutched at his gun for support and somehow he realised that the rest of the gun's crew were lying on the deck, dead or wounded. The third German salvo had found its mark.

Shells continued to thud into *Chester* in one continuous roar, but still Boy (First Class) John Travers Cornwell stood alone at his post, which was a most exposed one, calmly waiting for orders that never came. The first enemy salvo to hit the ship had cut all the electrical and voice-pipe communications from the Fire Control.

"STILL BOY (FIRST CLASS) JOHN TRAVERS CORNWELL STOOD ALONE AT HIS POST, CALMLY WAITING FOR ORDERS THAT NEVER CAME."

With her guns firing spasmodically as all control was cut off, *Chester* faced the fire of four German light cruisers for twenty minutes. Then she hauled off in an endeavour to lure the enemy within range of the Third Battle Cruiser Squadron, successfully dodging the hostile salvoes that were directed at her.

When the action eased off, Boy Cornwell was found at his post, mortally wounded, but 'carrying on' with his face towards the Bridge—he knew any orders would come from there. He was taken below, but the following morning he died, to be numbered with the two officers and thirty-three men who were killed in the brief but fierce action.

"His devotion to duty," stated the Captain of *H.M.S. Chester*, "was an example to all of us. . . . He stayed there, waiting, under heavy fire, with just his own brave heart and God's help to support him."

John Travers Cornwell was posthumously awarded the Victoria Cross.

JOHN F. C. WESTERMAN.

An enemy shell finds its mark.

By courtesy of] [*The M.G. Car Co., Ltd.*

G. E. T. Eyston driving a M.G. car on the Montlhèry track.

ON FIRE AT A HUNDRED MILES AN HOUR

A TINY racing car was roaring steadily round the track at Montlhèry, in France. It was the only thing moving on the wide expanse of concrete. It looked like a scurrying beetle.

As the car approached the replenishment pits the driver looked eagerly towards the group of mechanics and officials who had been watching the car. They were signalling him to come in. He stopped the car, and eased himself out from behind the wheel. He was tall and burly. He wore spectacles. He was Captain G. E. T. Eyston, the famous record breaker. He made straight for the time-keeper's box, to learn that he had just set up a new record, having driven his baby car at a speed of over a hundred miles an hour.

That was exactly what he had set out to do. Until that moment it had been thought impossible to reach such a speed in a car so small as the 747 c.c. M.G. Midget, even when equipped with a supercharger, as Eyston's was. He had proved that his critics were wrong. Another man might have been satisfied, but he was not.

"This is only a beginning," declared Eyston. "I intend doing better than this."

He was possessed by the restless spirit of all true pioneers. No sooner was one seemingly impossible objective gained, after intense trouble and effort, than he began to feel himself urged to strive towards another, still more difficult.

Having achieved a speed of a hundred miles an hour in a short burst, he decided that he would not be content until he had driven his baby car a hundred miles in an hour. There was a great deal of difference between the two feats. It was much easier to tune his little car up to a pitch at which it could be expected to reach a speed of 100 m.p.h. on a brief run, than to bring it to such a state of perfection that it would maintain the speed for a whole hour.

Many problems arose when he took the car back to England and went to work on it. For example, the alcohol fuel he used was so rich that it was difficult to keep the plugs 'alive' for longer than two minutes.

But failure could not discourage him. It urged him on to try still harder. After making some test runs on the Brooklands circuit Eyston decided that he was ready to make a bid for the new record. The Magic Midget was shipped back to Montlhèry, where the course was particularly suitable for baby cars.

On the day fixed for the attempt, Eyston and his mechanics were on the track at eight o'clock, tuning the car and giving it a last minute overhaul. About mid-day the timekeepers and other officials arrived from Paris. It was one o'clock before the preliminaries were over, and Eyston was ready to start his high-speed adventure. One of his assistants reminded him that he had had no lunch. Eyston shook his head. He was too eager to begin to bother about lunch. Besides, it was impossible to be sure that everything would go off all right. He had set his heart on putting up this new record, and he wanted to give himself plenty of time so that, if anything went wrong, he would have time to make a second attempt before the light waned.

Something was destined to go wrong. The hour before him was to prove one of the most hectic in his daredevil career. Although he was ready for almost anything when he started off on the first lap, he little guessed the amazing nature of the ordeal that was to crown his efforts. Right from the beginning he opened the throttle wide, and hurtled the car along the straight stretches of the track flat out.

TAKING THE CORNER.

As he started the first lap from a standing start, he knew that he would have to complete all the other laps at a speed in excess of a hundred miles an hour, in order to make up for his slow pace in the beginning.

Soon his rev-counter was indicating 6,400.

Each time that he came round the track, and down the straight, an assistant with a flag waved to him from opposite the time-keeper's box, to let him know whether he was doing a safe average speed. He circled the track for lap after lap at a steady 105 m.p.h. Every time that he sped past the time-keeper's box the flag waved cheerily, and he knew that all was going well.

On the straight the car was easy to hold, but on the sloped banking of the bends the sensation produced by riding at headlong speed in such a tiny machine was curious and alarming. Eyston himself described it as like " being on a pair of gigantic roller skates which wanted to climb higher and higher up the banking."

At times the air pressure in the fuel tank needed attention. Then Eyston would have to seize the pump handle and work it furiously until his shoulder ached and the gauge registered sufficient pressure. As the hour went by, Eyston kept a more frequent eye on the track clock, to see how many more laps he had to go.

In the excitement of getting off he had neglected to find out the exact moment that he had started, but he felt that he could judge the time close enough. He was soon to rue the fact that he had not made absolutely certain.

At last he realised that he could have only a few more minutes to go. His engine was still running perfectly. He felt immensely proud and pleased. The gallant little Midget had come through its test with colours flying. The only thing that troubled him was that the cockpit seemed to be growing uncomfortably warm. The gear-box was becoming positively hot. He could feel it through the soles of his shoes.

Once again he thundered past the time-keeper's box. At that very moment the engine began to set up an alarming clatter. Eyston caught his breath in dismay. What was wrong ? He had a sudden mental picture of a terrific crash at a hundred miles an hour.

He hurriedly put the gear lever into neutral, hoping that the momentum of the car would carry him once round the track. He was sure he couldn't have more than one lap to go, and even if he had to

By courtesy of] [*The M.G. Car Co., Ltd.*

After the fire had been put out.

get out and push the car the last part of the way, there was still a chance that he might have enough in hand to complete his hundred miles within the hour.

But even as these thoughts raced through his mind, he saw a flicker of flame from the engine.

The first flicker grew rapidly to a sheet of fire !

Flames roared up round the bonnet. Eyston stuck to his seat grimly, determined to hang on until the very last second in the hope of saving the record. The flames, blown backwards by the wind, ate their way under the dashboard. Soon they were licking into the cockpit, and running up the side of the seat. Eyston's clothes were smouldering. He could stay in the cockpit no longer. It was time to get out, and in a hurry. But Eyston is a big man. His friends used to chaff him, and say that his mechanics got him in and out of the Midget with a shoehorn.

He started to wriggle out of the cockpit. The soles of his shoes were almost burned through. His feet were scorched. With an effort he raised himself, squeezing backwards out of the cockpit while the car plunged on down the straight.

But even now, in spite of the fact that the car was well ablaze, he was determined not to abandon it until he was absolutely forced to. He wriggled back from the cockpit, and seated himself astride the tail of the flaming car, keeping one hand on the steering wheel.

It was impossible to reach the hand brake. There was no chance of pulling up. All that Eyston could do now was to steer the burning car as best he could, and try to finish the lap. The flames rose up round the steering column, and began to lick at his hands. With bitter reluctance Eyston realised that he would have to give up. A grassy bank came into view. It looked fairly soft and spongy. Eyston steered the car towards it. He hit it at top speed. The car jumped and bounced like a rubber ball.

Eyston threw himself from the blazing wreck. He came down with a thud on his shoulder. The force of the impact jarred every bone in his body. The grass wasn't nearly so soft as it looked. Eyston rolled over and over. He sat up dizzily. A friendly onlooker rushed to his aid, and helped him beat out his blazing clothes. He found, to his amazement, that his boots and socks were almost burned off his feet. He began to endure agonies. The onlooker pushed him into a car, and drove him to the First Aid station.

Meanwhile the Midget had gone on down the track, to finish the run on its own. As the blazing wreck came into the view of Eyston's mechanics, they rushed forward in alarm, and did their best to extinguish the flames, thinking that the driver might have been trapped behind the wheel.

For a few minutes there was panic. Eyston had disappeared, and no one knew what had happpened to him ! Then it was learned that he was safely in the First Aid station, being treated for his burns.

It was then that Eyston learned the most ironic news of all. He had actually completed his hour's driving, and beaten the record, before starting on that last nightmarish lap. Had he but paid closer attention to the clock when he started, he would have been spared his terrifying experience.

In his determination to finish if a finish was possible, he had imperilled his life. He could scarcely move. An ambulance took him to Paris, where he was forced to remain for a fortnight before he could be moved to England, on a stretcher, there to spend three more months as an invalid.

At the end of that time he was fit again, and making plans to smash still more speed records.

[*Vandyk Photo (L.E.A.).*

'BOBS': FIELD-MARSHAL LORD ROBERTS, V.C., K.C.B., G.C.B., etc.

THE LITTLE FIELD-MARSHAL

The Story of 'Bobs.'

ON the 14th of November, 1914, just behind the British lines, while the Battle of Ypres was proceeding, a little old man of eighty-two lay dying.

It was 'Bobs,' the greatest British soldier since Wellington. For sixty-three years, since he was a mere lad of nineteen in the Bengal Horse Artillery, he had been fighting his country's battles.

Names that have now been written deep in our history books recall some of the daring episodes in his long career—*Cawnpore, Lucknow, Delhi, Khyber Pass, Khandahar,* and *South Africa.* On a dozen fronts, from the Hindu Kush to the Modder River, he had fought his battles cleanly and had never suffered defeat. His brilliant strategy had won unstinted praise even from great soldiers in foreign lands.

Now, like a bolt from the blue, the fateful tragedy of the World War had come. This time, Britain, on land, sea, and in the air, had to fight for her very existence, and her greatest soldier lay dying within sound of the guns.

Weak and ill, in very bitter weather, the aged field-marshal, against his doctor's advice, had resolved to cross the Channel and talk once more with the British generals—the men he loved, the men he had trained on many a hard-fought field.

"I must see the boys again!" he said. "God help them!"

No one knew better than this valiant old fighter the ruthless power and strength of the German army. So he went to give his last words of encouragement and advice to the 'boys.' . . . Sir John French, Sir Douglas Haig, Pertab Singh who had brought over some of 'Bob's' old Indian regiments, and many others. They gave him a great reception.

But the effort was too much for him. On the evening of November the 14th, Field-marshal Lord Roberts, V.C., K.C.B., G.C.B., etc., joined the forces of the future. His end came as he had always wished it to come. Like his heroes, Wolfe, Nelson, and Sir John Moore at Corunna, he died on the field of honour. And the last thing he heard was the sound of British guns trying to stem the German invasion.

LORD ROBERTS CAPTURING THE SEPOY STANDARD AT CAWNPORE
AND THUS WINNING THE V.C.

He was the only soldier to wear two V.C.'s on his military tunic. Fifteen years previously, at the Battle of Colenso, his only son, Lieutenant Roberts, had died saving one of the British guns from the enemy.

Queen Victoria had posthumously awarded the V.C. to Young Roberts. But, as the youth did not live to wear it, the Queen *commanded* that the father should wear both decorations—his own V.C. which he had won nearly sixty years previously in the Indian Mutiny, on his left breast, and his son's V.C. on his right breast.

That was 'Bobs'! No British Tommy who had served under him ever called him by any other name. For forty years he was the idol of the British Army. And no Commander since the days of the Iron Duke ever evoked such hero-worship and such enthusiasm from the private soldier. The officers loved him no less. Even after Lord Kitchener had been made a general, he once said of his Chief:

"I should consider it an honour to clean his boots!"

The reason for all this hero-worship is not far to seek. Whenever Lord Roberts assumed a command, he made it his first duty to see to the comfort and well-being of his troops. To this end he made one suggestion after another to the War Office for innumerable reforms, and the removal of any injustice that pressed upon the troops. Even when he failed to move the War Office, the men understood, and appreciated his efforts.

Then there was the matter of his own personal courage. This little man 'Bobs'—though small of stature—had the heart of a lion. The story of his winning the V.C. during the Indian Mutiny is worth the telling:

After the relief of Lucknow, there had come that distressing appeal for help from Cawnpore, the scene of the terrible massacre of British women and children:

"Cawnpore hotly pressed by the enemy!"

Sir Colin Campbell with his famous Highland Brigade and other troops set off at the earliest possible moment across those burning plains. And with this relief column went Roberts, then a subaltern of twenty-five. Outside the beleaguered city they encountered the enemy. Roberts was foremost in that wild British charge. And in the mêlée he found himself separated from the rest. Seeing the Sepoy standard bearer just ahead, Roberts spurred his mount forward, cut down the man with his sword, and gripped the standard pole.

THE ATTACK ON THE HEIGHTS.

The wounded Sepoy, however, clung to the staff. And another Sepoy, turning savagely at bay, placed the muzzle of his musket within a few inches of Roberts's body and pulled the trigger. There was a click, but the musket missed fire. The Indian turned and fled. But Lieutenant Roberts, wresting the standard from the bearer's hand, galloped safely back with the prize. This was the daring, single-handed encounter which won for him the V.C.

His part in that heroic fight before the Cashmere Gate at Delhi, and a dozen other battles during the terrible days of the Mutiny, would fill a book. They cannot be told here.

The Indian Mutiny over, Roberts came back to England for a year. Although but twenty-six, he was already a veteran in fight. But when Queen Victoria had commanded his presence at Buckingham Palace, and pinned the V.C. upon his breast, the young soldier was ordered back to India.

His promotion was rapid now. From lieutenant to brevet-major and thence to major-general his rise to fame was swift. Here was a soldier of the Empire who had more than courage. He was found to be a strategist with great organising ability, always the mark of a great soldier. And in those troublous times in India and on the Afghan frontier Britain had need of him.

Once he had the power, he entirely reorganised and rearmed the Indian army. Then came a stirring event in his career, which of itself, would have given him an undying name. This was his famous *March on Kandahar*. In 1879 there had been trouble on the Afghan frontier. A British envoy, Sir Louis Cavagnari, had been murdered at Kabul, and a punitive expedition was sent through the mountainous regions of the Khyber to demand redress.

Peace was made at last, and a new Amir was placed on the Afghan throne. Roberts, who was in command of the Frontier Force, was about to return through the Khyber Pass from Kabul to India, when news arrived that all the wild, combustible tribes in south-west Afghanistan had broken out afresh, cut up a British brigade, and besieged it in Kandahar three hundred and thirteen miles away.

This was terrible news. And it was feared that a massacre would take place at any moment. 'Bobs' rose to the occasion. He was in Kabul where the question of the new Amir had just been settled. The road to Kandahar was appalling . . . scarcely a road at all. Mountain defiles, where the fierce tribesmen, armed with modern rifles

LORD ROBERTS'S MARCH FROM KABUL TO RELIEVE KANDAHAR.
From the picture in the Wantage Gallery.

supplied by Russia, must be negotiated. Flooded streams must be crossed, and if there was any delay, on their arrival, they might find the British garrison massacred.

" Seven miles a day will be good marching ! " declared one official.

" I will be there within a month ! " said Roberts.

The organisation of the transport was the chief difficulty. 'Bobs' worked it all out quickly :

The soldiers' kit was cut down from 30 lbs. to 24 lbs. per man. This had to include the greatcoat, for the nights in those mountainous regions were bitterly cold. Rations of flour, tea, sugar, rum and salt were allowed for thirty days. Every unfit soldier was left behind, and there were many sick and exhausted men.

Then, on the 11th of August, 1880, came the order " *Forward !* " The historic march on Kandahar had begun.

That day, ' Bobs ' and his little force launched out into the unknown. There was no means of communication with the rest of the world. Fanatical Afghan tribesmen, intent upon murder and loot, hung on their flanks and their rear. Every pack horse or mule, every exhausted, straggling soldier who could be picked off by these wonderful marksmen, lessened ' Bobs' ' army and reduced his supplies. But ' Bobs ' knew his job. And, although nearly every native transport driver deserted by the third day, and many of the animals were exhausted, the column went forward.

Reveille ! That was every morning at 2.45 a.m. Roll-call, inspection and breakfast followed. Then the tents were struck and all baggage packed.

March ! That was sounded at 4. a.m. Then the column advanced again.

Collecting fuel was a big task. A hot meal after an exhausting day's march became almost a luxury. But with ' Bobs ' there, the enthusiasm never flagged. There are a few men still alive in England and in the Dominions who endured that march. I have heard some of them tell the story. And it was always of ' Bobs ' they spoke. He was the inspiration that carried them through.

When the news reached England by the newly-laid cables from India that ' Bobs ' had set out on that perilous march, the very worst was anticipated.

" An impossible adventure ! " declared many people. " It ought to have been prevented. The whole force will be massacred ! "

And when for week after week no news came, all England became alarmed.

But still the column went forward. The intense heat of the day and the bitter cold of the nights took their toll of exhausted men and animals. But there was no talk of retreat. What happened? Did the column arrive in time to save the beleaguered garrison? 'Bobs'' promise had been: "*I will be there within a month.*"

Yes, he was there in twenty days. On the 31st of August, 1880, Kandahar was relieved. And shortly after his arrival, Ayub Khan, the Afghan rebel, and his army were utterly defeated and scattered.

So ended the historic march on Kandahar.

When the tidings reached England, 'Bobs' and his heroes were raised to the very pinnacle of fame. They had accomplished the *impossible*. Another wonderful page of endurance, heroism and grit had been written in the story of the British Empire.

More honours were piled upon 'Bobs.' He was soon made Commander-in-Chief in India. He held the post for seven years. Later still, he was raised to the peerage as Lord Roberts, but to the English Tommy he always remained 'Bobs.'

At length he came home to England after forty-one years' service in India and Burmah. He was then made Field-marshal and Commander-in-Chief of the British Armies. 'Bobs' was getting old now, nearly seventy. And some folks thought his life's work was done. But they were mistaken.

The unfortunate Boer War came next. It was an unhappy affair. Relations with the two Boer Republics in South Africa became strained. And while attempts were being made to find a peaceful settlement, the Boers declared war upon Britain in October, 1899, crossed the Tugela River, invaded the British colony of Natal, and invested Ladysmith, Kimberley and Mafeking.

The Boers were great fighters and wonderful marksmen. The small British Army rushed out to deal with them was hopelessly beaten. At Magersfontein, at Stormberg, and at Colenso the Boers held up the British advance with ease. There followed a deadlock.

Meanwhile, in Ladysmith, the British garrison were eating horse-flesh and it was impossible to relieve them. A feeling of the deepest gloom pervaded England. Nobody here had taken the full measure of the Boers.

Then a great cry went up: "Send 'Bobs'!"

LORD ROBERTS AND HIS STAFF ON THE VELDT.

LORD ROBERTS'S SON, LIEUTENANT ROBERTS,

E GUNS AT COLENSO AND WINNING THE V.C.

Very soon, not only London, but the whole country began to clamour for the old veteran to put on his uniform again and save England from dishonour. So ' Bobs ' went out to South Africa. Once out there, he entirely reorganised the Army on the spot, creating whole brigades of fast-moving mounted infantry, with light, horse artillery.

There followed a pause, and people in England waited anxiously . . . almost breathlessly.

LORD ROBERTS WRITING DESPATCHES IN A TRANSPORT WAGON.

"Will 'Bobs' fail us?" they asked. "He has never been defeated yet."

The Boers were exultant. It was great fun shooting down the *Rooineks* (English). They even talked about driving down through Cape Colony and making all South Africa Dutch. Ladysmith, Kimberley and Mafeking were still besieged.

Then 'Bobs' struck.

With amazing strategy and bewildering swiftness he struck in three places at once. The Boers were bewildered. Cronje, until now their great fighting man, with his commando of five thousand, was surrounded in a river bed, and compelled to surrender. This was on February 27th, 1900, some two months after 'Bobs'' arrival in South Africa. Flying columns dashed across the veldt. Kimberley, Ladysmith, and Mafeking were relieved.

Then 'Bobs' began his march upon the two capitals—Bloemfontein and Pretoria. Nothing could stop him. It was yet another victorious march. Both capitals were soon entered. Within five months of reaching South Africa, the British Army had entered the enemy's capital, and all the beleaguered towns had been relieved. And, although the Boer commandos now broke up into guerilla bands, raiding communications, harrying stock, and cutting off small garrisons, the war was practically at an end.

Leaving Kitchener to deal with the guerilla bands, Lord Roberts returned to England . . . his fighting days over. Honoured by his Queen, loved and esteemed by his fellow countrymen, 'Bobs' lived on another dozen years. Then, when he was eighty-two, and the great tragedy of the World War came, he took that little journey over to France to bid good-bye to the soldier boys he loved so well, and to die within sound of the guns.

When his brave spirit passed, the whole Empire mourned his loss. They brought his body home from France to lay his bones near to those of Wellington under the great dome of St. Paul's . . . that Valhalla of the brave Sons of Britain.

ROWLAND WALKER.

BRINGING UP THE GUNS.

THE SIEGE OF MOUNT EVEREST

Climbing the World's Highest Mountain.

LET us fancy that we are balanced on the side of a gully much steeper than a tiled roof and quite as slippery. A few feet above us it ends at an overhanging precipice; a few feet below it leads to another, and should we slip we would bounce once or twice in the gully and then fly helplessly through space to a glacier two miles beneath. Our route into this gully has been appallingly treacherous; nor can we get out except by the way we came, further progress being barred by a vertical buttress of naked rock. Nearly a thousand feet above us is the triangular summit which we had hoped to scale; furious winds sweep over it, and even here they chill us to the marrow. We have attained our present point only after many hours of tortoise-like progress, involving two or three deep breaths to every step; we seem to be suffocating for want of air, for although this is the airiest spot on Earth, there is so little oxygen in it that every breath is a gasp and every movement needs a stern effort. Daylight is fast running away; to stop in this gully too long means being benighted, with the certainty of death from freezing. Reluctantly we look once more at the distant triangle and turn away. We need not be ashamed of our defeat; for the mountain is Everest, and three of the world's greatest climbers have done in reality what we have just done in imagination.

Why climb mountains at all? you may ask. People do so because it is a thrill of the highest kind. It calls, moreover, for years of skill and training, besides large resources of pluck and endurance; one must also have an absolute trust in the judgment of one's companions, for often mountaineers are so placed that a mistake by one of them may hurl the whole party to its destruction. When men of this character perceive a noble summit, like Mt. Blanc, they say involuntarily: "Let's climb it!" and within one or at most two days the thing is done. But one cannot act like that on Everest; the mountain is so huge, so high and so remote, as to call for months of preparation, weeks of travelling, and much really hard work, before one comes in sight of it; and even then it must be besieged in form, just as if it were a fortress and the climbers the storming party. As a rule, when climbing parties have got to the foot of a glacier whence the mountain can be seen twelve miles away, they have been exhausted by a month's travelling through the deserts of Tibet ; they speak in hoarse whispers, their throats being parched and sore ; and any little weakness of limb or muscle is certain to break out within the next day or two. All their supplies have had to be carried up, by yaks and Tibetan or Nepalese porters. They have already spent something like £10,000. And yet, after all this labour and expense, they are still no higher than the summit of Mt. Blanc, and the *foot* of Everest lies thousands of feet above them, at the upper end of the winding glacier !

Let us assume that we have been with one of these expeditions. What do we do ? What do we see ? First of all, we establish a Base Camp at the glacier's foot ; and then we spend a week, or perhaps two, in getting over the twelve miles to its head, and in making a route up which laden porters can carry our stores to higher camps. Soon there are three such camps, No. III being the uppermost. From this point we may next take our bearings and discern what Mount Everest is like.

We perceive an enormous wall of rock and snow on our right hand. It forms one side of a huge pyramid, which terminates upwards in a sharply-cut line. The top of the pyramid has been sliced off skew-wise, and the cut edge runs slowly upwards, ending about two miles away in a rocky peak twice as big as the Great Pyramid of Cheops and looking not unlike it. On our left hand is a smaller mountain ; the gap between this and Everest is filled with an enormous mass of ice, one thousand two hundred feet high, facing us in a series of precipices and highly dangerous cliffs, except where deep cracks occur, down which to fall would mean instant death. This icy wall is the famous North Pass, the most practicable route up the mountain ; and not a step further can be taken until we have established a camp on its crest. Once there, however, we may reasonably hope to build higher camps, nearer and nearer to the final pyramid. But at a height of four miles above the sea, the labour of establishing that camp on the North Pass will be immense, especially as it must be safe for laden porters. We remember with a shudder that during one of the earlier expeditions a whole climbing party, porters and all, came to grief on this very wall ; for an avalanche fell upon them, seven men being killed. Up to this point, however, things have been relatively easy ; the route is now so well known that humorists among the 1936 expedition put up signposts on the glacier, bearing such words as :

"This way to the mountain!" and "Eggs can be obtained at the village on the right!"

Copyright] [Mount Everest Committee.

North Col. Camp and the north-eastern shoulder of Mount Everest.

As the 1922, 1924 and 1933 Everest expeditions all terminated at about the same point, whereas that of 1936 was ruined by snow and bad weather, let us follow the fortunes of the 1933 party, and watch how the great mountain was actually assailed.

They numbered sixteen British, led by Mr. Hugh Ruttledge, with about ninety hillmen from Nepal and Bhutan, many of whom had previous experience of this work ; the best and most loyal of these natives were known as the Tigers, a name that they had earned right worthily. At the Base Camp was a wireless transmitter, with an advanced station at Camp III ; whence T. A. Brocklebank, the old Cambridge stroke, was to carry a telephone wire right up the face of the ice wall. The weather since they arrived had been outrageous : snowstorms, gales, intense cold at night, added to the leader's anxieties by constantly delaying progress ; and even the arctic tents scarcely weathered some of the most furious blasts of wind. Besides the leader, there was a strong contingent of first-class climbers at Camp III ; including Messrs. Smythe, Shipton, Captain Birnie and Dr. Greene, who had conquered Kamet (27,450 feet—the highest successful climb on record) ; Wyn Harris, Wager, and Longland, the last a man who climbed vertical walls like a spider, just for the fun of the thing. Messrs. Crawford and Shebbeare were veterans of 1924, a disastrous year when two of the best climbers (Irvine and Mallory) had lost their lives near the summit.

For the sake of shelter, Camp III nestled under a mountain. It was now necessary to place a further camp (IIIA) right at the bottom of the ice wall, where the bitter winds poured down solidly from the Pass above, and where everyone was certain to be heartily miserable ; at this delightful spot the tents were blown flat more than once, but the work had to be done. First, ropes must be fixed and steps cut up the least steep precipices. This pioneering was accomplished by Smythe and Shipton, not without some narrow escapes. At one place they were stopped by a vertical wall of ice, with no hold whatever. Here Shipton drove his axe into the cliff ; then Smythe stood on it and drove in a stake as high as he could reach ; he cut foot and hand holds, and hauled himself up on to the stake. As he did so it gave way, and he was within an ace of a nasty tumble. Eventually, however, he got to the top, fixed a stake in the sloping ice above, and tied a rope-ladder to it ; thus even the porters could ascend it, once the way had been made for them. This would not be easy work, even at sea level ; it was terrible labour more than 20,000 feet up on Everest, with a stinging wind trying to tear one from one's hold.

A PERILOUS MOMENT.

After a week's hard work Camp IV was established on a sheltered ledge two hundred feet below the Pass ; it was only five yards wide and thirty yards long, with a profound crack on the wall side and a sheer drop of a thousand feet to the green tents of Camp IIIA on the other. From time to time small snow avalanches fell from the Pass above, mostly tumbling into the crack ; but they became so bad later that a new camp (IVA) had to be built, up on the narrow and gale-torn crest of the Pass itself. To Camp IV Brocklebank carried up his wire, and Ruttledge even installed a typewriter there, on which he tapped out his dispatches. The messages were telephoned to Camp III, relayed to the Base Camp, then wirelessed to Darjeeling one hundred and eighty miles away, again relayed to Calcutta, and in six hours from being issued by Ruttledge were on the printing machines of the *Daily Telegraph* in London.

Despite much bad weather, lulls at times permitted the programme to continue. A strong climbing party led the porters up the cliffy mountain wall, fixing Camp V almost on the crest of the truncated pyramid, 25,700 feet above the sea ; this was one of the highest camps ever made, but it soon had to be abandoned again—temporarily, at any rate ; and during the retreat more than one man lost a finger from frostbite. Captain Birnie, weary of the plodding descent, attempted a glissade down the snowy slope which led to Camp IVA ; but he lost his position, rolled over, and went down head first, on a course which must have taken him over the edge, to be dashed to pieces far below. Without a moment's hesitation, Da Tsering, one of the Tigers, dived across his feet, pulled him up, and the two men stopped their fall in a patch of soft snow. But for this brave act Birnie would undoubtedly have perished.

From Camp V onwards the mountain side is like the tiled roof of a house, with smooth, rocky slabs sloping outwards and downwards ; it offers no foothold except to nailed boots, and when glazed by ice was so slippery that even nails scarcely sufficed and the climber had to depend on his sense of balance ; should he slip, he would slide for a few hundred feet and then take one gigantic leap to the glacier 10,000 feet below. The top (not so smooth now that it was seen at close quarters) was a jagged ridge, narrow, and with an ice-sheathed wall on the far side, which even a fly could scarcely scale ; and as the top was swept by a strong and extremely bitter west wind, the climbers were compelled to keep along the dangerous slabs. The

Copyright] [*Mount Everest Committee.*

At the foot of North Col.

summit, still nearly a mile away, was now defended by two great black walls, known as the First and Second Steps; a way had to be found round or up these, if success was to be achieved.

Meanwhile the climbers shivered or slept, according to their temperament, in Camp IVA, while the wind tore at their tents and threatened to hurl them down bodily on those of Camp IIIA below. On the 28th of May it improved, however; so Wyn Harris, Wager, Longland and a party of fresh porters set out once more, re-established Camp V, and the next day went on and made the last camp, No. VI, at 27,400 feet, on the slabs, nearly five and a quarter miles above the sea. Here Harris and Wager remained; to Longland fell the responsible task of getting the porters down again safely. He left in the camp four sleeping-bags, provisions for three days, and cooking utensils. Longland now spent an unforgettable time; for the mountain was so vast, and the visibility so poor, that he soon imagined that he had lost his way, and was haunted by the fear that he would lead his trusting followers over the precipice. Soon a puff of wind arose; another moment, and all of them were enveloped in whirling masses of powdery snow. The wind became a gale. Speech was impossible, and they reeled in the wind like drunken men. Nevertheless, Longland kept his head. He clustered the porters close together;

made them stop and be counted at frequent intervals ; and when they wanted to sit down from sheer weariness, urged them to go on, well aware that to sit down now would be to rise no more. All this time he had the paralysing thought at the back of his head : "Am I taking the right direction ?" His fears proved groundless ; but many of the party were frost-bitten before they stumbled into the tents of IVA, while Longland's face and beard had become a mass of icicles. One porter, old Kipa, who had been there in 1924, insisted that he was dead, so dazed was he ; and it was a considerable time before he could be persuaded to the contrary !

Copyright] [*Mount Everest Committee.*

Mallory and Norton approaching their highest point (26,985 feet) May 21st, 1922.

Everything was now set for the final assault. Wyn Harris and Wager were to make it ; and Smythe and Shipton, who had pushed up to Camp V, were to follow them if the first attempt failed. The first pair, leaving Camp VI on a bitterly cold morning, managed easily to pass the First Step, but the second proved insurmountable. It was a huge limestone cliff more than one hundred feet high, overhanging in places ; and they could not even reach its base. They therefore kept below it along the slabs towards a great gully which was white with soft snow, and which seemed to breach the cliff.

To get down into this gully was a perilous task, for the slabs were narrow and the angle steeper than ever ; there was neither foothold nor handhold. Once in the snow, they found it impossible to get out on the far side, where a cliffy buttress barred the way ; at the top of the gully was another unscalable cliff, and a third just below them dropped, as already stated, right down to the glacier two miles below. They noticed a minor and easier gully beyond the buttress, but by no device could they reach it. Both men felt that to linger here would mean a topple over and a quick death ; so they turned back, the summit mockingly clear and serene above them. They had reached about 28,200 feet above sea-level ; thus, there was nearly a thousand feet to climb and about half a mile between them and success.

During this exploit they found an ice-axe resting on the slabs, which had certainly belonged to the missing climbers of 1924 ; it was in perfect condition, but it told little of their fate, except to imply that they had slipped on the slabs and had been carried down to their doom. The axe, being light and flat, would readily rest where the owner must inevitably roll over and over, perhaps clawing madly at the rocks in a last effort to save himself, until he took the last fatal leap.

When Harris and Wager reached Camp VI, Smythe and Shipton had moved up to that point. The former pair now continued down to Camp IVA to recuperate ; and as they neared the camp, Harris, who was suffering from the peculiar lassitude due to great heights, tried like Birnie to slide down ; but he, too, changed direction and in an instant was heading straight for the precipice. Cool as ever, he pressed his ice-axe close to his breast and slowly dug the point into the snow, until the braking effect pulled him up on the very edge of the abyss ; then, badly shaken by this narrow shave, he made his way sideways to where his comrade could help him.

Smythe and Shipton spent a cheerless night at Camp VI. Owing to the impossibility of finding a level spot on the mountain side, the tent floor overhung, and the stones beneath were sharp and hard. Shipton had the lower berth ; and, said Smythe : " I spent the night in rolling on top of Shipton, and Shipton spent the night in being rolled on by me." Nor was the next day much better ; for they woke to find a gale howling along the slabs, making their canvas tent flap as if it were mad, and trying vainly to hurl it and its occupants far below.

At night the wind went down, however, and early next day they set out ; only for Shipton to succumb with stomach trouble after going a short distance. While the sick man struggled back to the tent, Smythe went on and eventually got into the gully where Wager and Harris had been. On the far side, he drove his axe into a crack in the buttress and found a foothold on a small ledge ; but the rock suddenly gave way beneath him and crashed off down the gully. In the same instant he grasped the axe ; fortunately it held, and thus by a miracle his life was saved. Despite this escape he persisted, next trying a lower level ; but the snow was thigh-deep, and to clear it away step by step until one was sure of a foothold proved too exhausting even for Frank Smythe. He, too, turned back, defeated, and without much difficulty regained the camp. During all the time that he was alone he had the curious delusion that a second person was beside him on the mountain ; but it left him as soon as the little green tent came into view.

Shipton had now improved enough to descend ; Smythe, however, decided to stay one more night at the highest camp on Earth. Soon after they parted a terrific storm broke out, and poor Shipton, bewildered, dazed, speechless, and exhausted, had the greatest difficulty in getting down alive ; nor was his comrade in the tent much better off, for if a single rope had given way, *his* end would have been certain.

This storm decided the fate of the expedition. Next morning the slabs, mantled with snow and ice, looked more treacherous than ever ; and Smythe wisely decided to descend for the present. He had not gone far before the storm broke out anew. He was forced to his knees, and even then, with blinding snow whirls all around him, and with feet and fingers slithering about on the ground, he often had to anchor himself down by his axe, otherwise he would have been blown away.

When he reached the lower camps, Ruttledge decided to take the whole expedition down to the Base to recuperate ; and although they made a further effort a few days later, it was only to find that much of the hard-won route up the North Pass had been obliterated by avalanches, while clouds of snow from the raging monsoon were mantling Everest in the purest white.

For that season, as on every other assault—1921, 1922, 1924, 1936—victory had gone to the mountain.

B. Webster Smith.

[Cribb.

The hidden gun comes into action.

HEROES OF THE "MYSTERY SHIPS"

QUEER things were those "Mystery Ships" of the Great War. And if ever there was a note of comedy amid the countless tragedies of those dark days, we may find it mingled with the cunning patience and heroism of some of the 'Q' Ship exploits.

No mousetrap in any pantry was ever baited with such artful cunning to entice the midnight marauder as were some of the British "Mystery Ships." Beneath the innocent disguise of a tramp steamer badly in need of a coat of paint, an ordinary merchantman, a trawler, or even a sailing ship, the 'Q' Boat would venture out along the shipping routes, asking for trouble. Sooner or later the *trouble* arrived and the 'U' Boat commander found to his intense disgust that he had encountered one of those nasty ships that could hit back. Then, if the 'U' Boat could dive quickly enough and get out of range, it might live long enough to fight again. If it didn't, then, as a rule, it

[Sport & General.

The forward hatch of a " Mystery Ship " (gun concealed).

took its last long dive. There were occasions, however, where the 'Q' Ship itself never returned. Some of them vanished without trace, with never a word about their last great fight with the enemy.

The official pages of the *London Gazette* for 1917 and 1918 contain, with some precise, reliable details of these daring episodes, the awards which were granted by King George V to many of the 'Q' Ship heroes. Here is one taken at random from the *London Gazette* of July the 20th, 1917 :

> *The Award of the Victoria Cross* has been made by His Gracious Majesty to Lieut. Ronald Neil Stuart, D.S.O., R.N.R., and Seaman W. Williams, R.N.R., O.N. 6224 A, for gallant service in action with an enemy submarine on June the 7th, 1917.

Behind that brief announcement of the award of the coveted trophy lies a story which is worthy of the best traditions of the British sea-dogs in the days of the Armada peril. The " Mystery Ship " in this case was the *Pargust,* and although but a few cold facts follow in the *Gazette* recording the incident, the imagination of the reader quickens as he visualises the adventure which happened on board both the German submarine and the British 'Q' Ship on that eventful day.

At this time the pitiless submarine campaign was daily growing worse. Germany was becoming desperate. Unfortunately, five weeks previously, the German admiralty had discovered the secret of the 'Q' Ships, when U 39, after an encounter with the British "Mystery Ship" *Prize,* had escaped. That was on April the 30th, 1917. The U 39, presumed sunk, managed to limp home to the German port of Emden. Then, for the first time Von Tirpitz learnt with amazement of this new English devilry. Instantly every 'U' Boat on the high seas was warned by wireless code message. And from that moment the work of the British "Mystery Ships" became more deadly and difficult than ever.

The message, which was just a jumble of misplaced letters like the following, reached the 'Q' Ships quickly:

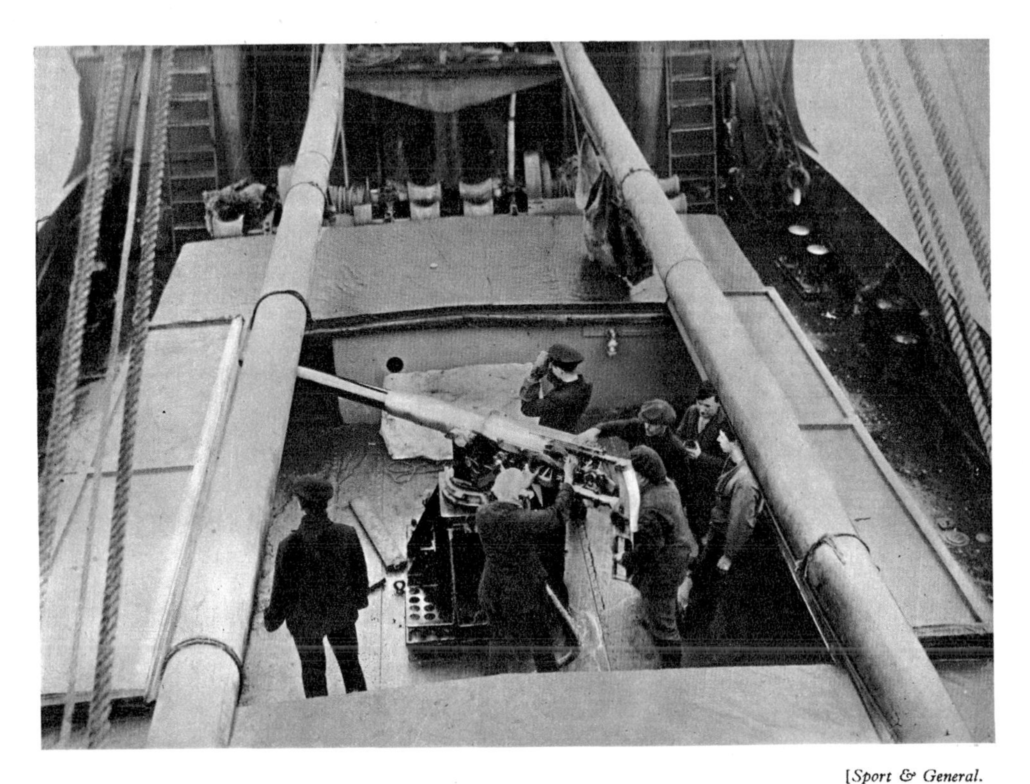

[*Sport & General.*

The gun revealed. This was only one of many appliances which made these innocent-looking vessels a terror to U Boats.

dhs phnu mfs z hdyscs o fknm rzk, x

Its significance, however, was considerable. The British secret was out, for the message, decoded, ran as follows :

British decoy ships heavily armed with hidden guns, posing as innocent merchantmen, now patrolling shipping routes.

Whether that particular wireless message was one of the 50,000 'intercepts' decoded by the British Admiralty in the famous cipher wizards' Room Forty, I cannot say.

The 'U' Boat commanders out on the prowl, however, received it quickly, and altered their methods of attack accordingly. This startling news also called down upon the 'Q' Ships a special brand of vengeance, which probably accounts for the complete disappearance of some of the "Mystery Ships" with their entire crews. From now on, to every 'U' Boat commander, any tramp steamer, collier, liner or fishing smack he encountered, was a possible 'Q' Ship whose bulwarks would collapse, and whose hidden guns would deliver a smashing broadside once the submarine came within range.

So it happened that on this particular day, the 7th of June, 1917, this sorry-looking tramp, the *Pargust,* thrashed her way slowly along one of the British shipping lines as if her best endeavour were to deliver some mixed, general cargo at a distant port, and earn her owners a respectable dividend. Members of the crew lounged about the deck in their greasy, sea-stained clothes. There was no brass work twinkling in the sun, no apparent haste to carry out orders from the bridge. Not a trace of the H.M.S. about the ship.

Nevertheless, keen-eyed watch-dogs aboard the 'tramp,' from hidden observation posts, searched the horizon and the surrounding seas narrowly for a periscope, or a tell-tale streak of oil. No enemy was seen.

Yet all this time the stalkers were being stalked. And a German submarine which had glimpsed the *Pargust* crept in submerged towards its prey.

"BOATS WERE LOWERED AND THE *PANIC PARTY* MADE A RUSH TO GET A SEAT."

"THE LAST BOAT WAS LOWERED AND PULLED AWAY."

"Another verdammt Britisher, Herr Kapitan!" announced the first officer. He had glimpsed the *Pargust* through the periscope.

"Not a 'Q' Ship, Herr Leutnant?"

The first officer gave a quiet shrug. The periscope was sent up again for a brief spell, and another observation taken.

"She may be—!" the Kapitan decided. And as weather conditions favoured the 'U' Boat, he resolved to try conclusions with the *Pargust*. "Anyhow she carries one gun aft, which makes her an armed ship."

The 'U' Boat commander had seen the very obvious gun which the *Pargust* carried at her stern. One small gun, if mounted aft, so that it could only be used in self-defence while a merchant ship was trying to show a clean pair of heels, was now permissible. Had the Kapitan known that this *solitary* gun was a dummy, he might have been more wary still . . . suspecting worse things. Apparently he didn't. So he gave the order:

"Action stations!" And the torpedo tubes were manned.

Greatly daring, the Kapitan went closer in, manœuvring the 'U' Boat to bring the *Pargust* broadside on. Then the order was given:

"Fire!"

It was at this moment that a streak of white on the surface of the sea was glimpsed from the *Pargust*.

"Torpedo!" came a warning shout from the lookout. But it was too late. The tin fish had got home.

> "*A shadow like a shark—I saw the damned torpedo glide;*
> *Like a sunken reef it jarred her ribs.*
> *It ripped her loaded side*
> *As the killer rips the mother whale in the red Behring tide.*"

The explosion that followed was terrific. The starboard lifeboat was smashed. The hole in the ship's side caused the engine room to fill, and No. 5 hold quickly flooded. A slight mist having crept up and the surface of the sea being choppy, had given the 'U' Boat a chance to get close in before she unloosed her deadly charge.

Yet this was only the beginning of the big adventure. And although it really seemed as if the *Pargust* was doomed, the quiet, unruffled courage of the sea-dog on the bridge seemed in strange contrast to the *apparent* panic of the crew.

A few sharp, short orders were rapped out. One of them was: "Abandon ship!"

Boats were lowered, and the *panic party*, having rehearsed their part many times, made a rush to get a seat, then pulled away from the doomed ship. That panic seemed all very real. The men were wearing all kinds of rig, as though the *Pargust* had been manned by a crew of dagoes. As the last boat was lowered and pulled away from the ship under the command of Lieutenant Hereford, the submarine was observed some four hundred yards away on the port beam.

"There she is, sir!" came a warning cry from one of the boats.

"Where away?"

"On the port beam, sir!"

The periscope of the 'U' Boat had been glimpsed some four hundred yards away. But the Kapitan was still suspicious.

"Is this one of the verdammt British 'Q' Ships or isn't it?" he asked his first officer.

After the barest glimpse of the torpedoed ship, the periscope disappeared again. Fritz was taking no unnecessary risks. He had evidently got 'Q' Ships on the brain. He wanted to see the other side of the *Pargust*, now apparently doomed.

"The fight was over now, only the work of rescue remained."

There followed a few moments of suspense and uncertainty. The gun crews lying flat on their faces aboard the *Pargust* must have had a trying time. At any minute, their ship, filling rapidly, might sink beneath them.

The 'panic crews' in the boats paddled about waiting . . . waiting . . . for the sea pirate to reappear.

" The *Pargust* did not founder that day. Yet it seemed a miracle that she kept afloat."

" Periscope ! " came a hail from the second boat. " Passing right astern, sir ! "

And there she was. The ' U ' Boat had passed right astern of the *Pargust,* first toward the starboard beam, then back toward the port beam again, finally breaking the surface not far from the lifeboats.

There was another dramatic pause.

Then the conning tower opened. Two German seamen raced out on to the wet, slippery deck of the submarine, and pointed a machine gun at the lifeboats. Other men emerged. The Kapitan felt now that he had nothing to fear from the waterlogged, torpedoed *Pargust.* The next instant the German ' U ' Boat commander received the biggest surprise of his life.

" *Let go !* " came a vibrant voice from the deck of the *Pargust.* And down the speaking tubes the order reached the ears of the hidden gun teams.

In a flash, gun screens, false bulwarks and shelters collapsed. At the same instant, the white ensign, the fighting flag of Britain, soared aloft, and every available gun aboard the *Pargust* opened fire and raked the German ' U ' Boat.

"Crash—crash—crash—!"

The submarine had been lured so close in that every shot told.

The 'U' Boat's side and conning tower were ripped. Black smoke and oil poured from her deck and torn plates. Wounded and unwounded men scrambled out of the conning tower, then held up their hands in token of surrender.

"Cease fire!" ordered the merciful British skipper.

Then followed a dilemma. It looked now as if the *Pargust* and the 'U' Boat would sink side by side. The 'U' Boat's engines were still running, however. She was evidently intact below. And seeing the condition of the torpedoed ship, the 'U' Boat commander believed that, though he couldn't submerge, he might yet crawl away.

He resolved upon one desperate bid for freedom. Listing heavily, the 'U' Boat made off across the bows of the *Pargust,* her speed gradually increasing. But there was no escape that way.

"Fire!" came the order a second time. Then, amid another halo of bursting shell, the 'U' Boat's list became greater. Her stern next began to sink. She filled rapidly, then disappeared with one man clinging to her bows, and others struggling in the waters.

The fight was over now. Only the work of rescue remained. But the 'U' Boat had moved so far to windward during the last ten minutes of the fight, that the 'panic party' in the boats had to pull hard to save even the few survivors who remained afloat. That done, the saving of the *Pargust* was the next task. Urgent wireless calls for help were sent out to the patrols. And very soon afterwards the look-out on the torpedoed ship gave a welcome hail:

"Smoke on the horizon—!"

Very soon three smokes were observed. No enemies this time but two American destroyers and a British sloop racing to the rescue.

The *Pargust* did not founder that day. Yet it seemed a miracle that she kept afloat with her engine-room and boiler-room flooded. Aided by the patrols, she managed to limp back safely to port.

* * * * *

This little adventure which befell the *Pargust* that June day in 1917, was only typical of innumerable incidents which happened to other 'Q' Ships during the pitiless submarine blockade of Great Britain. The *London Gazette,* in which all the King's awards were announced for such heroic service, is full of similar episodes and honours. Every man aboard the *Pargust* that day was a hero . . .

"THE 'U' BOAT DISAPPEARED WITH ONE MAN CLINGING TO HER BOWS AND OTHERS STRUGGLING IN THE WATER."

[Fox Photos.

A German 'U' Boat.

even those members of that serio-comic 'panic party' which made that 'frantic rush' for the boats . . . as though the very sight of a 'U' Boat had unhinged their minds with terror.

But what of the gun crews who remained behind, crouching in their narrow, confined spaces, with the *Pargust*, as they really believed, sinking under their feet ?

They were doubly heroes.

They waited for what . . . another torpedo to blow them sky high ? The ship to take its final lurch and carry them with it down into the depths ?

No ! They waited just to fight it out to a finish with the sea pirate, and, incidentally, to turn an apparent defeat into a daring victory.

Every one of these men deserved the V.C. But as that was impossible, two men were chosen, by common consent I believe, for the coveted decoration. They were Lieutenant Ronald Stuart, and Seaman W. Williams.

ROWLAND WALKER.

HUNTING MUSK OXEN

" Marvin was sent back for more petrol."

BY SLEDGE AND DOG TEAM OVER THE POLAR SEA

How Peary Reached the North Pole.

BESIDE the north-west corner of Greenland runs a " Street of Adventure " as famous as any in the world. It is really not a street at all, but a *strait*, for it has the huge frozen plateau of Greenland on one side and the ice-clad hills of Ellesmere Island on the other. For almost its entire length of 350 miles, the " pavement " on each side is made up of thick, more or less horizontal ice-shelves, frozen fast to the land, but broken into countless platforms at different heights above the sea : this is the dreaded " ice-foot." Between the two pavements is a " roadway " of ice cakes or floes that are almost always in motion ; ten, twenty, even fifty feet thick, and sometimes frightfully rough and piled into mounds, they sweep up and down at the will of the powerful tides, carrying along bergs and berglets with resistless force, so as to bear down all opposition. Other bergs get caught in the narrow channels between fixed and moving ice, or stranded behind frozen points, or turned completely over, their green surface a mass of spires and pinnacles, like vehicles caught in traffic jams or upset by an accident.

This Street of Adventure starts in Baffin's Bay and ends in the vast, land-free Arctic Ocean; hence it has long been a favourite line of approach to the North Pole; and Kane, Markham, Greeley, Peary and many another bold explorer have driven their ships into that treacherous road, though few have ever got through at all, while none have got through unscathed. Ships have been crushed there like eggshells at the tap of a spoon; and the survivors, dragging their heavy boats on sledges, starving, ill-provided with footgear, weakened by scurvy and sickness, have made terrible marches towards the Eskimo and Danish outposts far to the south. Many, alas! have fallen by the way; and piles of stones, their rude memorials, may be seen by the adventurous traveller as he wends his way north.

Into this Street of Adventure there came, in August, 1908, the stout steamer *Roosevelt*, under the command of Captain Bartlett, bearing Commander Peary, a few white men, a number of yellow-skinned, black-haired Eskimos and their families, besides one hundred and fifty noisy and quarrelsome Greenland dogs, *en route* for the Pole. To both Peary and Bartlett it was a Street of Adventure indeed, for only three years before, in the same vessel, they had had many a narrow escape from shipwreck here. Little wonder, then, that the broad-shouldered Newfoundland skipper sat aloft in the crow's nest, while his leader, much older and more spare of frame, was spread-eagled

An Eskimo building an igloo.

Mondiale] [*Dr. Trenkler.*

Afloat on an ice floe in the Arctic.

out on the rigging high above the deck ; from both commanders there issued short, sharp orders that brooked no questioning—" Hard aport ! " " Full speed ahead ! " " Full speed astern," " Dead slow," as they navigated the ship in and out among the cracks of the sea ice which filled their " roadway."

Robert E. Peary was a true Arctic hero, the most remarkable of all, perhaps, among that heroic and hard-bitten tribe. He had originally visited Greenland twenty-three years before on a holiday, had been smitten with the lure of the Arctic, and had determined to make exploration there his life-work. He had made wonderful sledge journeys across the plateau overlooking the " Street," covering many hundreds of miles simply to prove that Greenland was an island ; and though defeated time and time again, at last he had succeeded. His next task was to attack the Pole—that elusive spot, the goal of so many efforts and cause of so much heroism and suffering for nearly four centuries ; separated from all land by four hundred and fifty miles of ice-clad ocean, it was a magnet which lured him on to extraordinary but fruitless efforts. He was defeated ; but each defeat only stiffened his resolution the more ; neither foul weather, impassable lanes of open water, broken sledges, nor shortage of food could diminish his ardour for the task of his life—to reach the Pole. In 1905 the *Roosevelt*, then a new ship, advanced through the Straits as she was advancing now, to their extreme end, where she found a safe haven at Cape Sheridan. After a winter of polar gloom, a series of well-organised parties set out, Peary himself coming last; each of the others was to support him for a certain distance and then return, handing over its surplus food and fuel: by these means only was it possible to provide supplies for the long journey of two months' duration. Up to a point everything went well. The lanes of deep sea were safely crossed, the difficulties of ice ridges, storms, broken sledges, were overcome as they arose, and at last, in the spring of 1906, Peary crossed the 87th Parallel. He was farther north than any other man had been. But his supplies were exhausted, and he was forced to turn back into a maze of treacherous water channels, cakes of thin ice, with stormy weather which drove him far out of his homeward course and nearly landed him and many of his people at the bottom of the sea. They were thoroughly and completely beaten; and the dreadful anxiety of getting the *Roosevelt* back through the ice-filled Straits would have sufficed for the lifetime of any other man.

[*Topical (L.E.A.)*.

Peary in his Arctic outfit.

Peary was now

[*Fox Photos.*

Encamped under the bows of the ship.

fifty years old. He had spent his best years in that desolate, inhospitable waste. He had left there eight of his toes, and had permanently weakened his leg by breaking it in two places. But he would not give up : it was not in him to admit defeat. Again he organised an expedition ; and again he sailed those dangerous waters, on his sixth and greatest expedition. This time, however, he had to conquer or abandon the contest, beaten by the weight of years.

At the entrance to the Straits he had picked up his Eskimos, members of an Arctic tribe for whom he had the warmest sympathy, and who in turn were attached to him. He relied upon these little people to provide him with sledge-drivers and dogs ; and by selecting the best of them, and promising them such luxuries as rifles, whale boats and even tents if they reached the Pole, he made sure of their allegiance. The men were employed on deck in preparing specially long sledges of a pattern designed by Peary himself ; and their womenfolk, who were intended to remain at the ship's quarters while the expedition was away, now found ample work in sewing up skins to make fur clothing and boots, the attire most suitable for that bitter, wind-swept region. Lest you should think it was all ice and snow, however, I may say that in sheltered valleys, for a few brief weeks of summer, grass rose shoulder high ; buttercups and many other northern flowers flourished ; and even the droning of bees was heard. Upon this herbage (which was buried under the snow in winter) lived the gnarled and hardy musk-oxen ; hares there were in plenty, too, arctic foxes, polar bears, seals, and walrus ; and upon all these creatures the Eskimo relied for food. You can understand then how extraordinarily valuable a rifle was in an Eskimo's eyes, and how he would undergo almost any hardship to obtain one.

Meantime everything was kept ready for quitting the ship at a moment's notice ; and the boats were fully stored for swinging overboard. Yet the first part of the passage proved easy, for on one wonderful day's run they notched one hundred miles of the Street of Adventure, without so much as an incident worth noticing. This open water soon gave place to a turbulent flood of floes, surging to and fro in the channel, crunching, screaming and groaning as if they were possessed ; between these dangerous neighbours and the shore ice the *Roosevelt* was slowly guided, taking refuge behind a promontory whenever a particularly heavy mass threatened her ; or charging down bodily on each side of a crack alternately, so as to open it ; or, by means of a sudden access of steam to the engines, dashing violently

[*Fox Photos.*

Looking after the dogs.

[*Wide World Photos.*

On an ice-bound shore.

forwards for a few moments, so as to break down a bridge by main force. It was dangerous work, so dangerous that for a week neither the leader nor Captain Bartlett slept out of his clothes. As they reached the last and narrowest place, Robeson Channel, they got caught in the stream of moving floes, and the *Roosevelt* was "kicked about as if she had been a football." Suddenly a big floe picked up the berg to which she was anchored as if it had been a toy, thrust it aside, smashed the ship's bulwarks, and drove her aground. Immediately afterwards another berg split in two, and a fragment weighing five hundred tons at least crashed down within a foot or two of the rail. In order to loosen the rough icy bed beneath her, Peary ordered the ice to be dynamited; but although the explosion shook everything in the vicinity, the ship remained fast. At last, however, she was warped off, and soon afterwards came to the same safe anchorage at Cape Sheridan where she had lain in 1905-6. The first part of Peary's fight was won.

A new colony sprang up as if by magic at this loneliest spot in the world. Huts were built on shore, the dogs were turned loose, the decks cleaned down, coal and stores landed (in case the ship should be crushed by some unlucky storm), and everything made as snug as possible for the long winter night. Parties of both whites and eskimos were sent out in search of walrus or musk-oxen, for fresh meat was rightly regarded by Peary as a vital means of fighting the explorer's scourge, scurvy. Just before the light failed, too, a party carried stores to Cape Columbia, a promontory ninety miles further along the same coast, and from which the take-off to the Pole would be made. There remained now nothing to do but pass the winter as comfortably as possible, busied with the thousand and one details of next year's journeys ; and the four months' night slipped away without incident. There was one anxious moment, however, at its commencement ; for on the night of November the 12th Peary was turned out of his bed by a violent shock, as the floes in the moving water near by attacked the ice to which the ship was fast, and began to pile up on it. He rushed on deck, to find huge blocks of ice piling up alongside to a height of thirty feet ; and as they pushed along, the edge of a great floe touched the starboard beam. Something had to go, and the *Roosevelt* began to tilt landwards. Peary called all hands on deck and had every fire extinguished. Slowly and surely the ship was upheeled ; but at last the pressure ceased, leaving her at this uncomfortable angle for the rest of the winter.

On the 15th of February, 1906, Bartlett left the ship with the first Polar party, finding his way to Cape Columbia by lantern light. Next day went another party under Dr. Goodsell, the surgeon ; two days later Macmillan, with Peary's Negro servant Henson, set out ; then Borup, a young Yale student ; then Professor Marvin ; and last of all, Peary himself left the ship on February the 22nd. By the end of the month they were all at Cape Columbia, a great mass of rock and ice which fronted the Arctic Ocean.

They could see nothing but ice stretching out to the horizon ; and they knew that it reached on in one vast mass for the whole of the four hundred and thirteen miles which lay between them and their goal. A short distance offshore it became rough and moundy, due to the pressure of the floes against one another ; and these mounds, which were apt to stretch like ramparts straight across the route, were a serious obstacle, straining sledges and men alike, and wearing out the dogs. From Cape Columbia the sky was light ; Peary dreaded the day when it might become dark, for that would indicate lanes or leads of open water, a still more potent source of delay.

Pioneers were sent ahead to find the best route and to break down the worst obstacles by force ; they were aptly called the Pickaxe Brigade. It had been intended that each party in turn should tackle this arduous work, but most of it fell on Bartlett's party. When he was well away, the remainder set forth successively, to the cracking of whips and the shouts of the drivers, as they strove to control the bounding, struggling dogs. Over the flat places they made fine progress; but it was another story when they sweated, tugged, swore, and nearly broke their shoulders in tugging the five-hundred-pound sledges over the hummocks! There were twenty-eight sledges in all, manned by seven whites and nineteen Eskimos, with one hundred and forty dogs. For huts snow igloos were used: the native home of the Eskimo, built of snow blocks in half an hour, and sufficient to protect men when tents would be blown to shreds. The igloos were made of blocks overlapping one another towards the centre, and cunningly shaped to fit; a special " key-stone " block filled the roof; and a snow-slab couch was built at one end within. The door was completely filled in with snow. Such was the nightly home of Peary and his men; with twenty feet of sea ice beneath them and the cold ocean water under that.

[Topical.

Huge blocks of ice piling up on the ship.

The parties had only been two days on the march when they ran into trouble, a lead of open water a quarter of a mile wide barring the way; nothing could be done but to stand and look at it, praying that the wind or tide might close the crack. Meanwhile, the rough jolting on the hummocks had produced numerous leaks in the petrol tins, so Marvin was sent back for more ; for without this vital item of fuel Peary might just as well have remained on the *Roosevelt*. As soon as the crack closed, the others pushed on ; but they were still only forty-five miles from the Cape when they were again held up—this time by the dreaded Big Lead, a permanent crack where the deep sea begins, and where Peary had nearly lost his life three years before. The water, black and steaming, showed no signs of being iced over sufficiently to bear ; and five whole days passed at its edge, while supplies were being eaten up, and Peary and Bartlett were tramping about in vain efforts to master their anxiety. Another source of worry, too, was that Marvin had not returned with the fuel. A week passed, ten days, eleven days, and still there was no possibility of crossing. The Eskimos, easily disheartened, became frightened, and some of them feigned illness and were sent back ; but Macmillan kept the others together by diverting them with games and exercises. On the twelfth day, the lead at last closed just enough for the sledges to be rushed across it ; but still there was no sign of Marvin. The same night the floors of the igloos swayed as the tide urged the ice up and down, the floes creaking and groaning most dismally. Nevertheless Peary went on. On the evening of the thirteenth, just as the igloos had been built, an Eskimo shouted, "Dogs are coming!" It was Marvin with the fuel ; and so another anxiety vanished.

Next day Dr. Goodsell was sent homewards with two Eskimos;

Central Press.

The tilted stump of a tabular iceberg.

Macmillan, Borup and Marvin successively followed him; meanwhile Peary had been gradually moving to the front, like a prudent general, supervising everything.

There were accidents, of course. Once two of Borup's dogs fell into the water, and might have dragged a sledge load of food and fuel after them had not Borup, who was immensely strong, sprung forward and pulled them out bodily by the traces. On another occasion Peary and Bartlett were camped side by side, when the ice broke at night right between the two camps; leaving Bartlett's party on a block which was rapidly drifting away, while Peary's block seemed in danger of foundering. Peary got his own people on to a firmer floe; and then, fortunately for everybody, Bartlett's floe drifted close in to this piece, the sledges were rushed to the edge, and as the ice-blocks momentarily touched were hauled across to Peary's side. An instant's hesitation at such a moment would have spelt disaster.

[*Wide World Photos.*

The Peary Monument, Cape York, Greenland.

Finally, Bartlett turned. The gallant skipper had reached 87° 4′, a latitude never attained by any man till then. It was the first of April. There remained only Peary himself, his loyal servant Henson, and four Eskimos—Egingwah, Seegloo, Ootah and Ooqueah; all fit and well, with five sledges and forty dogs. By forced marches, driving his people to the limit of their strength, Peary hoped to accomplish his aim; and how he actually did so all the world knows. Five days later an observation showed him to be at Latitude 89° 57′; a few miles more, and all roads led south. He was at the top of the world; the dream of centuries had been realised, and the prize was his. Excited though he was, however, he fell asleep from sheer exhaustion. But as soon as he had recovered a little, and had verified his position, he photographed his people, with the Stars and Stripes planted on a convenient hummock. A sounding disclosed that the ocean here must be two miles deep at least. Then came thoughts of home.

Peary well knew that a single southerly gale might imperil all their lives by opening impassable leads in the ice ; and he knew, too, from Nansen's awful experience how difficult it was to cross sea ice in summer, when it was a mass of melting sludge. He therefore insisted upon forced marches all the way back to Cape Columbia ; and by taking chances and straining their powers to the uttermost, this was actually accomplished. Early on the morning of April the 23rd they were back at Cape Columbia, having done in sixteen days a journey which on the outward track took thirty-eight ; this wonderful feat was largely due to the outward route still being visible for most of the way.

Unhappily, Peary's men did not have the same good fortune. Several of them missed the outward route ; but they all got back alive, except poor Marvin, who was drowned at the Big Lead.

All the parties now returned to the ship. By the first week in July the *Roosevelt* had regained an even keel. A week later the ice near her began to loosen ; and on the 18th of July she started homewards. Just a month later the Eskimos were dropped at Etah, their summer camp ; and so ended the most successful Arctic adventure on record.

B. WEBSTER SMITH.

[*Wide World Photos.*

The unveiling of the Peary Memorial by Captain Bob. Bartlett and Mrs. Marie Peary Stafford at Cape York, Greenland.

[Cribb.

"Early in the morning the two battle-cruisers steamed quietly into Port Stanley."

NO SURRENDER

The End of the Raider Squadron.

ON the 2nd of November, 1914, bad news reached the British Admiralty in Whitehall. A small British squadron, off Coronel in the Pacific, on the previous afternoon, had encountered the famous German raiding squadron under Admiral von Spee. And without waiting for reinforcements, Admiral Cradock, the British commander, although the enemy had double his own gun power, had instantly challenged and fought the enemy. The result was from the first a certain defeat. The utmost Admiral Cradock could hope to accomplish was to cripple the German armoured cruisers *Scharnhorst* and *Gneisenau*, which had played such havoc with British merchant shipping on the eastern Empire routes.

In this Cradock failed. The heavy guns of the German armoured cruisers pounded the *Good Hope* and the *Monmouth* to pieces. But so long as a single gun could be fired, the smaller British cruisers fought on. After two hours fighting the end came swiftly. And soon after sunset, both the *Good Hope* and the *Monmouth*, battered and blazing, went down with their flags still flying. That night, in a rising gale, and ten thousand miles from home, even while the battleship *Canopus*, two hundred miles away, was racing to the spot, Admiral Cradock with 1,650 British officers and seamen went down to their death.

It was a gallant but useless sacrifice. It left the German raiding fleet as strong as ever. And Admiral von Spee resolved to round Cape Horn, raid British mercantile shipping in the Atlantic, then fight his way home. What followed was one of the big dramatic surprises of the Great War.

Ten days later, two British ships, the *Invincible* and the *Inflexible*, having been detached from the British battle fleet in home waters, silently disappeared into the evening mists of the North Atlantic. They were mystery ships under the command of Admiral Doveton Sturdee. And nothing more was heard of them for several weeks. Their mission was the best kept secret of the whole war. South and still south they sped at great speed. Ten thousand miles they covered on their mysterious errand in twenty-six days, without any wireless 'chattering' *en route* to raise the suspicion of the German spies who were known to be in every South American port.

Early on the morning of December the 7th, the two battle cruisers steamed quietly into Port Stanley, in the Falkland Islands, that

[*Photopress.*

"A great cloud of smoke hung over Port Stanley.'

[*Topical Press.*

H.M.S. Inflexible.

farthest southern outpost of the British Empire, with the coal in their bunkers almost exhausted.

" Coal ship ! " was Admiral Sturdee's first order.

In the harbour were other British ships, the *Canopus*, and several small cruisers, the scattered remnants of Admiral Cradock's squadron which had been sweeping the South Atlantic.

Strange as it may seem, that very day, while the British ships were coaling, the powerful German raiding squadron which had sunk the *Good Hope* and *Monmouth* were rounding Cape Horn, and Admiral von Spee was holding a council of war on his flag ship.

" Tomorrow, we will attack the British naval base in the Falklands," said the admiral. " We will first destroy the wireless station, sink any ships in the harbour, land an armed party, seize the Governor and destroy the stores. What do you think, my captains ? "

" Nein, nein, Herr Admiral ! " replied the captain of the *Gneisenau*. " We may be running into a hornets' nest."

The admiral gained his point. It was generally felt that if this old British colony could be destroyed before the squadron commenced raiding the Atlantic shipping on its way home, the moral effect would be considerable. England would feel that a staggering blow had been struck at the Empire. So Von Spee headed for the Falklands.

At 8 a.m. next morning, the 8th of December, while the British ships were still busy coaling, from the signal station on the little hilltop above the harbour came the message :

" *Smoke stack away to south-east!* Then, shortly after : " *A four-funnel and a two-funnel man-of-war in sight, steering northward !* "

It was the advance party of Von Spee's squadron scouting for any sign of the enemy.

" *All ships raise steam !* " was Admiral Sturdee's first order.

Twenty minutes later from the signal station on Sapper Hill came a further message :

" *Another smoke column to the southward !* " This was Von Spee's main fleet now heading direct for the harbour entrance.

By this time a great cloud of smoke hung over Port Stanley, for the two battle-cruisers were raising steam quickly by oil fuel. At all costs the British admiral was anxious to keep from the approaching enemy the secret so well kept of the arrival of the two battle-cruisers.

" Once they see the tripod masts of the *Inflexible* and the *Invincible* over the neck of the land, the secret will be out. Von Spee will turn tail," he said. As a bait, therefore, Sturdee sent the *Kent*, a weak British cruiser to the harbour entrance.

The big, black smoke cloud puzzled the Germans. They knew warships were present. But not yet for another hour did they suspect the presence of the two battle-cruisers.

" They're burning the oil fuel and the coal stores to prevent capture ! " the enemy decided. That same thing had happened when the raiders threatened Papeete.

Then one of the German officers aboard the *Gneisenau*, peering through his glasses, declared that he could make out tripod masts . . . the sure sign of battle-cruisers.

" No ! " decided his captain. " There is only the *Canopus*, and a few weak cruisers of the *Kent* and *Glasgow* class." And he wirelessed this information to Von Spee in the rear squadron.

At 9.20 a.m. Von Spee had not yet guessed the truth. The game was his . . . so he thought.

" Action stations ! " was ordered on the German fleet.

The *Scharnhorst* and the *Gneisenau* drew closer in and trained their guns on the wireless station. The next moment Von Spee

[*Topical.*

H.M.S. Invincible.

received his first surprise. The *Canopus*, though invisible, her fire directed from the hilltop, sent a 12-inch shell over the neck of land and very nearly hit the *Gneisenau*.

The second surprise was bigger still. The Germans were opposite the harbour mouth now, some eight miles distant, and their leading ships were about to attack the *Kent*, sent there as a decoy, when, to their horror, they saw the British fleet coming out to engage them. And now for the first time they saw the two battle-cruisers.

Von Spee's order was instantly sent out to all his ships :

" Battle not to be accepted ; concentrate with course north-east ; high speed ; steam to be raised in all boilers."

Instantly every German ship turned tail. This time, however, there was no escape for the squadron which had been raiding British merchant shipping in the Pacific for seventeen weeks. There were no friendly harbours, no neutral ports. The day was early, the weather fine and clear, and the whole South Atlantic lay before the two fleets. Willy-nilly, Von Spee had to fight.

Admiral Sturdee left his two slower ships, the *Canopus* and the *Bristol,* in harbour, as other vessels had been reported further south —either transports or colliers. The British squadron, therefore, was as follows: *Invincible, Inflexible, Carnarvon, Glasgow, Cornwall* and *Kent.* Von Spee's squadron consisted of the *Scharnhorst, Gneisenau, Nurnberg, Dresden* and *Leipzig.*

Once out in the open, from the British flagship there flew the order: "*General Chase.*"

It was a stern chase and a long one. It lasted nearly three hours, by which time the enemy had changed his course almost to due east. But this time the British ships had the advantage of speed. The enemy ships at first were hull down. Gradually not only the masts, but the funnels and the bridges began to show above the horizon. The distance between the ships lessened.

Just at this time, however, a wireless message was flashed from the *Bristol,* which had been left at the Falklands, saying that three more enemy ships had been sighted off Port Pleasant. These were

[*Central Press.*

The German warship *Gneisenau.*

Topical.

The German warship *Scharnhorst.*

believed to be the colliers or transports in attendance upon the German fighting fleet, and instantly Admiral Sturdee flashed back the order to *H.M.S. Bristol:* " *Destroy them!* "

For another hour the chase continued. Then, at 12.47 p.m., the *Inflexible* opened fire. It was a trial shot. The enemy was within range, and from the British flagship the signal was made:

" *Engage the enemy.*"

The German admiral, seeing that flight was now impossible, resolved to fight. And the *Scharnhorst* and *Gneisenau*, which held gunnery records for the whole German navy, began to reply. Very soon the battle became general. But the British gunners, with their 12-inch shells, found the mark first. The *Gneisenau* was hit twice, although the range was still some eight miles.

By this time both battle fleets were in line ahead, and almost parallel. And for two hours at long range the ding-dong of battering fire continued at intervals. The *Gneisenau* had her wardroom wrecked and her third funnel shot away. Then the heavy British shells, piercing her armoured gun casements, wrought terrible destruction.

Next it was seen that the *Scharnhorst* was on fire in many places. Great holes in her side showed a dull red glow of flame.

At this point, Admiral von Spee, knowing that his two best ships were doomed, ordered his three cruisers *Dresden, Leipzig* and *Nurnberg*, to leave the battle line and escape. Instantly Admiral Sturdee ordered the *Glasgow, Kent* and *Cornwall* to follow and destroy them.

By this time three separate battles were being fought—the first between the battle-cruisers, the second between the light-cruisers, the third between the *Bristol* and the colliers . . . all out of sight of each other. The big fight, however was between Admiral Sturdee's ships and those of Von Spee.

The *Scharnhorst* was the first to sink. At 4.17 p.m. the end came suddenly. The big ship, her guns silenced, her hull battered to pieces, listed heavily to port. The list increased until, lying on her beam ends, with her flag still flying bravely, and with never an offer to surrender, she sank. The *Gneisenau* still fought on, but the steam was pouring from her escape pipes now; all her guns but one were out of action, and she was badly on fire.

"*Cease fire,*" ordered the British admiral. And the German was asked to surrender. But there was no surrender. The flag which had flown at her truck had either been shot away or hauled down. But the flag at the peak still flew aloft And with her single gun she still continued to fire. The British admiral had no other course but to

[Cribb.

"As a bait Sturdee sent *H.M.S. Kent.*"

[*Central Press*.

"For two hours, at long range, the ding-dong of battering fire continued."

sink her. And a little later she capsized and sank. Then the British ships dashed in to rescue the survivors. There were some two hundred men struggling in the icy water. Lifebelts were thrown and boats lowered as the ships came up. Many were rescued. The *Invincible* alone took one hundred and eight survivors on board, fourteen of whom died through exposure. These were buried at sea next day with full military honours.

Meanwhile, after a stern chase and a running fight, two of the German cruisers, the *Leipzig* and the *Nurnberg*, had been sunk in the second fight. But night was falling now and the weather thickened, so the *Dresden* escaped in the dark

For three months she played hide-and-seek in the great waters of the southern Pacific. But on March the 14th next, the *Kent* and *Glasgow* caught her off the Island of Juan Fernandez and sank her in five minutes.

As for the other ships, they turned out to be colliers laden with coal for the German ships, and the *Bristol* took off their crews and sank them while Sturdee's battle-cruisers were hammering Von Spee.

A queer thing happened while this great battle was in progress. A great four-masted sailing ship which had rounded the Horn loomed up like a ghost-ship. It was a French ship which had been at sea since July and whose captain did not even know that war had broken out. Slowly she sailed on almost through the battle line, and for a brief space, the British ships ceased their fire lest she should be hit. Then the strange ghost-ship vanished into the misty horizon.

That was the end of the famous German raiding squadron. All the German ships were sunk. Von Spee and two of his sons went down with their ships. And nearly three thousand of Germany's best seamen and gunners were killed or drowned. The British total losses were six killed and seventeen wounded. And although the German gunners made thirty hits, no British ship was seriously injured.

Let us pay tribute to a gallant foe. Von Spee's men fought as Cradock's men had fought. The word '*surrender*' had no place in either battle. All the ships went down with their flags flying.

It was a bitter sacrifice.

Many of the British and German naval officers who fought that day had been friends. But in 1914 the two countries were at death grips. And when the rescued Germans came aboard the British flag-ship, Admiral Sturdee first congratulated them on their magnificent courage, then, with deep, human feeling in his words, he sympathised with them on the loss of their admiral and his brave seamen.

Let us do honour in our hearts to the heroic seamen of both Cradock's squadron and Von Spee's, who now sleep beneath those southern waters ten thousand miles from their own shores.

ROWLAND WALKER.

A "C" class light-cruiser in action at the battle of Coronel.

By courtesy of] [" *Flight*."
A test pilot wearing helmet, goggles and oxygen apparatus for an altitude test.

TEST PILOTS

Men Who Risk Their Lives in the Cause of Safety.

BEHIND every great achievement in aviation, whether it be the establishment of a new record, the winning of a great air race or the production of some remarkable new type of aeroplane, there lies the work of the Test Pilot, representative of a little-known body of airmen upon whose skill and daring aeronautical science depends for the translation of theory into practice.

Because their work is concerned with flight-testing of new and untried types of aircraft and is necessarily often of a secret nature, the public knows little of these pilots, who, above all others, are supreme masters of the flying art.

Every aircraft-constructing firm employs one or more test pilots whose duty it is to take each new machine into the air for the first time and submit it to searching trials before it is finally handed over to its purchaser. The days are past when the first trial of a new aeroplane was an occasion for speculation—and not a little appre-

By courtesy of] [" *Flight.*"

Testing the " Bristol " high-altitude monoplane in which Squadron Leader Swain beat the world's height record.

hension. To-day, aeronautical science has advanced sufficiently for aircraft to be built with the certain assurance that they will fly. But it still remains for the test pilot to discover, at the risk of his own life, just how well or how badly they fly. If there is the slightest tendency for a machine to become unmanageable at certain speeds or in certain attitudes, as is sometimes the case with new designs, then it is on these defects that the test pilot must concentrate, purposely forcing his machine into the most perilous positions so that its " vices " may be detected and remedied.

To do this work with success the test pilot must be more than a highly-skilled airman. He must be a specialist with a wide knowledge of aircraft design and construction. He must possess a temperament that is neither too highly-strung nor yet too slow for instant reaction in moments of emergency. He must also be able not only to detect a fault in a machine's behaviour in the air but also capable of putting his finger upon its probable cause. Above all, he must be a man of high courage.

The tests to which a new aeroplane is submitted vary according to the type and to the duties for which it is intended. Large commercial air-liners, which are not intended to withstand the excessive strains imposed by aerobatics or fighting manœuvres, will undergo less searching tests than a military aircraft which must be able to support the greatest stresses that a pilot fighting for his life could possibly impose upon it. It is among the test pilots of military aircraft, therefore, that one finds the highest expression of the art of test flying and, in this country, the most searching tests to which it is possible to submit an aeroplane.

Fast diving and turning tests at speed, aerobatics, slow flying, climbing, spinning and ease of recovery from abnormal positions, all form an essential part of the "breaking in" of new types of fighting aircraft. Included in these tests, for British fighters, is a terminal velocity dive in which the aeroplane is dived vertically, with the engine full on, from a great height. In the course of these dives test pilots of the latest types of single-seater fighters now being built for the Royal Air Force have attained speeds well in excess even of the present world's speed record of 420 miles an hour. A strong constitution, iron nerves and perfect judgment are needed for a "T.V." dive, as it is called, and the moment of greatest danger comes when, on nearing the ground and with the machine travelling at its

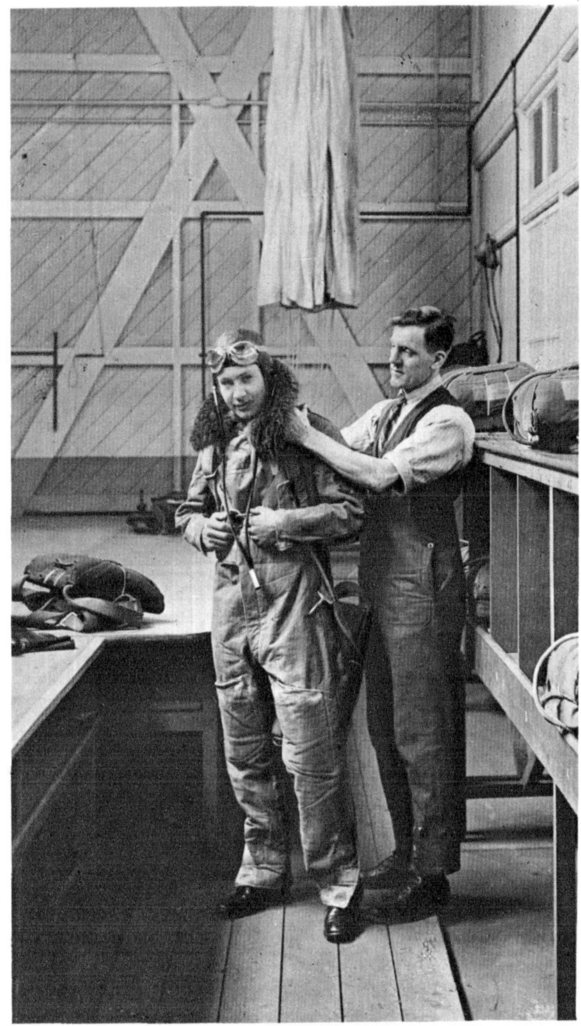

By courtesy of] [*The Bristol Aeroplane Co. Ltd.*

FITTING A PARACHUTE.

The test pilot's safety, and often his life, depends on the accurate working of his parachute.

" DOWN, DOWN, DOWN—250, 300, 350, 400 MILES-AN-HOUR."

greatest velocity, it must be eased out of its headlong dive into level flight. It is then, if ever, that a machine will break up under the terrific strains imposed by the sudden alteration in course, and cases have been known where wings have folded back and broken off under the mighty pressure of the air, leaving only the wingless body, like some monstrous projectile, to continue its hurtling plunge to destruction.

Some idea of the amazing speed attained in the course of these "T.V." dives is afforded by the recent experience of a test pilot while diving a new type of R.A.F. fighter from 25,000 feet to 5,000 feet. Nearing the end of the dive he shut off his engine and was amazed to discover that even with his engine off his speed was so great that the propeller was actually being rotated by the rush of air at a greater speed of revolutions than the ordinary maximum with the engine on. In other words, he was travelling so fast that even the full use of his 800 h.p. engine could not have increased the speed of his headlong dive by a fraction of a mile.

Presence of mind and the ability to act quickly but calmly in a sudden crisis are essential attributes in the make-up of a successful test pilot. Emergencies in high speed flying seldom allow of second thoughts, and not every test pilot is likely to be as fortunate as Flight Lieutenant C. S. Staniland, the famous test pilot of the Fairey Aviation Company, who was recently concerned in one of the strangest experiences that can ever have befallen an airman.

In the course of testing an experimental type of R.A.F. two-seater fighter, Staniland suddenly discovered that it was impossible to extricate it from a headlong spin which, even as he struggled with the controls, developed into the still more dangerous "flat spin," in which the aeroplane rotates in a horizontal plane as it falls earthwards with increasing momentum.

When it was evident that the machine was totally uncontrollable and a crash inevitable, Staniland decided to escape by means of the parachute which every test pilot carries. Standing up in the front cockpit he leapt overboard, only to find himself, a second later, sprawling *in the rear cockpit,* while the mach e continued its wildly-whirling descent. More surprised than alarmed, Staniland considered this amazing experience, realised that he had been jerked back by centrifugal force and decided that by jumping over the opposite side of the machine he would be thrown off at a tangent and would drop clear of the falling 'plane. Now less than 1,500 feet from the ground,

[*Central Press.*

FLYING UPSIDE DOWN.
Not a stunt machine, but a powerful "Gloster Fighter" employed on Home Defence.

he dived overboard for the second time and landed safely by parachute some distance away from the field in which his machine had been reduced to a tangle of splintered wreckage. An hour later he was in the air again carrying out spinning tests with a similar type of machine.

Another instance of presence of mind was afforded by Captain H. S. Broad in the course of an early trial of the De Havilland "Comet" monoplane which subsequently won the MacRobertson Race to Australia. A large crowd of spectators had gathered on the aerodrome to watch the trials and on their conclusion they were horrified to see Broad preparing to land with the wheels of the machine still tucked away inside the wing-cavities where they are housed when in flight to reduce wind resistance. Frantically they waved arms, hats and handkerchiefs, while others, more enterprising, hurriedly detached spare-wheels from their cars and brandished them in warning to the pilot. At the very last moment Broad opened up his engines and climbed away to return a few moments later for a perfect landing with the wheels down and in position.

To his relieved audience Broad calmly explained that after carrying out a series of tests with the wheels alternatively up and down he had become uncertain of their position and had purposely simulated a landing in order to watch the reaction of the spectators! Had this method proved inconclusive, he added, he would have flown low down and tried to secure the necessary information by observing the shadow cast by his machine on the ground against the sun.

Equally enterprising was the action of another test pilot whose rudder-control cable snapped just as he was about to land a small type of cabin monoplane in a strong wind. Fortunately there was a door on either side of the cabin and by directing his passenger slightly to open one or other against the wind stream as required, he was able to keep the machine straight enough to effect a safe landing.

Among the most arduous tasks of the modern test pilot are the ascents which have to be made to the cold and rarified air of high altitudes in order to ascertain the maximum height or "ceiling" attainable by a new type of aeroplane or engine. Clad in electrically-heated clothing and wearing oxygen-breathing apparatus, he may climb, in the space of a few minutes, from a summer temperature on the ground to the arctic coldness of great heights, a lonely figure in space, dependant for his life upon the successful functioning of his oxygen system.

By courtesy of] [" *Flight.*"

A "Hawker Fury" doing a "terminal velocity" dive through the clouds.

By courtesy of] ["*Flight.*"

C. S. Staniland, a well-known test pilot.

A famous R.A.F. test pilot, Flight Lieutenant S. L. G. Pope, was once carrying out one of these altitude tests above Norfolk, when suddenly his oxygen supply failed and he immediately fainted. As he lost consciousness he dropped forward on to the control-stick, sending the machine plunging downwards in a steep power dive at a speed of nearly five miles a minute. Five thousand feet from the ground the denser atmosphere revived the pilot. Instinctively he eased the machine out of its dive and landed, suffering from nothing worse than violent head- and ear-aches. Examination of his machine showed that the sudden failure of his oxygen supply was due to his having accidentally started off on his climb using his reserve supply instead of the much larger main supply. Turning this on, Flight Lieutenant Pope insisted upon taking-off again and completing the test climb upon which he had been engaged.

Deliberately to invite disaster is sometimes required in test flying, and some little time ago Captain M. Piercey, an experienced test pilot and former war "ace," undertook a series of tests, the sole object of which was to try to pull the wings off a fighter 'plane when it was travelling at a speed of nearly 300 miles an hour. Several unexplained accidents had occurred to this type of machine, the cause of which was believed to be due to a "flutter," or excessive vibration of the wings, which, at very high speeds, might be sufficient to fracture the spars and collapse the wings.

To confirm or disprove this theory, Captain Piercey was sent up in a similar machine with a parachute and instructions to impose the greatest possible strain upon the framework—and to watch the results. Climbing to the machine's maximum "ceiling," he nosed it over into a dive with the engine full on and waited. As the machine quickly attained its maximum velocity a slight vibration of the wing-tips became apparent. Rapidly it increased in intensity and spread along the surfaces until soon both planes were flexing visibly under the strain to which they were being subjected. Still the pilot sat and watched.

Then the control-stick began to thrash from side to side, bruising his hands as he fought to hold the machine in its headlong dive. The bracing wires on the wings slackened and snapped, and slowly but quite perceptibly, the wings began to fold back towards the body. A last scribble on the writing-pad strapped to his knee and Piercey leapt from the cockpit and dived overboard. Almost simultaneously the wings parted from the machine with a loud report and fluttered earthward, narrowly missing the now-opened parachute in which the pilot was descending with precise details

By courtesy of] [" *Flight*."

A Royal Air Force test pilot about to go up.

of the sequence of events leading up to the final breakage of the wings. His cool and expert observation under circumstances where the average pilot would have little time—or inclination—for scientific observation had been the means of tracing the cause of the mysterious weakness which might otherwise have cost the lives of a number of pilots.

Even test pilots, however, are sometimes literally caught bending, for there is on record the case of one who, having dropped his notebook on the floor of the cockpit, unstrapped his safety-belt to bend forward and retrieve it. As he did so the machine suddenly heeled over and he was thrown out. Being some two thousand feet up at the time, he was able to release his parachute and land, safely but face downwards, in a ploughed field, his machine falling into some trees half a mile away.

Report has it that when the inevitable crowd of spectators arrived, the pilot, after wiping the mud from his face and lighting a cigarette, calmly enquired: "Has anyone round here seen my kite?"—adding, as an afterthought—"I've just fallen out of it!"

T. STANHOPE SPRIGG.

By courtesy of] ["*Flight.*"

Starting up the engine for a test flight.

[*Topical Press.*

An early type " B " class submarine.

FORCING 'THE NARROWS'

"YOU are to proceed up the Straits and torpedo anything you can find on the way, then return and report on the going ! "

" Very good, Sir ! " acknowledged Lieutenant Norman Holbrook, R.N., commanding submarine B-11.

Such, in brief, were the orders given to Lieutenant Holbrook and his reply, but the words meant more than they implied to the uninitiated. The Straits, of course, referred to the narrow strip of water between the Ægean Sea and the Sea of Marmora, twenty-seven miles long, three and a half of which were less than a mile wide. The Straits change their direction twice : at "The Narrows" between Kilid Bahr and Chanak from north-east to north and at Nagara sharply from north to east. Furthermore, currents from the Ægean and Black Sea rip through this narrow sea-way, and in 1914 very little was known of the underwater set and drift of these currents.

To add to these difficulties, the Turks were known to have laid rows of mines somewhere off Kephez Bay. There were also heavy and alert shore batteries thickly placed on each side of the Straits, besides swarms of patrol ships.

Lieutenant Holbrook's submarine, B-11, was built in 1906, so she was not one of the latest boats when she left the shelter of the Fleet on December the 13th, 1914, to force "The Narrows." But she had reached the Ægean Sea under her own power—no mean achievement in those now far-off days—yet to expect her to penetrate the most difficult of sea-traffic routes held by the enemy seemed hopeless. There was one great thing in her favour, however. Lieutenant Holbrook, her commander, who was only about twenty-five years old at the time, was a tried and trusted submarine officer of long and useful experience.

On December the 13th, 1914, B-11, with three officers and thirteen ratings on board—all picked volunteers—cramped in her confined space that was further reduced by masses of machinery—electric motors, Diesel engines, dynamos, compressors, air tanks, torpedo tubes, torpedoes, pumps, batteries and the thousand and one control wheels and 'gadgets'—slipped away and began her hazardous passage.

Before she was in sight from the land she submerged with only the tips of her periscope showing above the water, and proceeded slowly so that no eagle eye should spot the tell-tale plume of spray. She poked her nose past Cape Helles and Sedd-el-Bahr at the entrance, only able to show her periscope for split seconds at a time.

In the control room, Lieutenant Holbrook watched depth gauges, compass and periscope, giving occasional orders to the helmsman and the seamen on the hydroplane controls. Of all the men on board, her commander was the only one who had occasional glimpses of the outside world. The rest could only carry out the orders that affected them, trusting blindly to the judgment of their 'Skipper,' knowing full well the dangers that lurked outside and waiting—waiting for anything.

Again and again they heard the thud of propellers passing over them or close by as hostile patrol boats raced about. Depth charges had not been invented at the time, but there were other things that could send them to the bottom for good. There was a deep silence in the submarine—a silence only broken by the hum of the electric motors and an occasional order.

"Raise periscope!" The command came suddenly. "Stop! Lower periscope!"

The orders came in quick succession, then Lieutenant Holbrook made a sound of satisfaction. They had covered the long reach to Kephez without being seen by the shore batteries or patrol boats. So far, very good: but the worst part was before them. They were on the edge of the reported minefield. Kephez Point was on the starboard beam. Three miles further on was the first turn and "The Narrows"!

"Down to one-fifty feet!"

"Down to one-fifty feet, sir!" The order was repeated back

"In the control-room Lieutenant Holbrook watched depth-gauges, compass and periscope."

calmly, after the fashion of the Royal Navy, although all on board realised what was happening. With something like thirty feet of water under their keel, they were going to attempt the dive under the minefield and they knew that the slightest touch on one of the unseen globes would result in the end of everything as far as they were concerned.

Dead slow, B-11 crept forward, steering by compass only in unknown waters. Was there any current drift forcing them into the Bay of Kephez ? They did not know, but waited, listening for any sound that might give them a clue. Again and again they imagined they heard the rasping sound of a mine's mooring cable scraping by the side of their ship. That was all right, provided that none of the wires fouled the hydroplanes or other projections on the submarine's hull. That had to be chanced.

In the control room, Lieutenant Holbrook watched clock and compass. After several long-drawn-out minutes he had no accurate idea of his position. He only knew that his ship's head was pointing north-east. He could only wonder if the currents had shifted his vessel—they were strong at this point. He hung on until he judged he must be clear of the mines. Then it was necessary to try to fix his position.

" Before she was in sight from the land, she submerged."

" Up to fifteen feet ! " he ordered suddenly. " Steady with her. Stand by for a crash dive ! "

A crash dive meant that the submarine would dive as quickly as engines, hydroplanes and ballast tanks could act. It imparted a severe strain on ship, machinery and crew and was only used in extreme emergency, but his men stood by calmly as the order echoed through the small vessel.

Up went B-11, to stop quietly at the desired depth. There was a certain amount of sound to be heard above the hiss of the water discharging from the ballast tanks—sounds that spoke of other craft in the vicinity. All hands waited.

"Raise periscope! Stop!"

A split second later Lieutenant Holbrook's voice was heard again. There was a slightly exultant ring about it.

"Lower periscope! Easy ahead! Flood the for'ard torpedo tube!"

Joyfully the men carried out the orders that meant only one thing. Their skipper had seen a target worthy of their attention and sufficiently important to merit disclosing their presence.

[*Central News.*

Lieutenant Holbrook at the time of his exploit.

Stealthily B-11 crept forward, cautiously raising her periscope every few seconds. Lieutenant Holbrook had seen right ahead the bulk of a large, grey-painted, two-funnelled vessel flying the Turkish flag, when he first raised the 'eye' of the submarine. The ship was the old Turkish battleship *Messudiyeh*!

At length B-11 was within eight hundred yards of the warship. Taking one last look through the periscope, Lieutenant Holbrook gave the seemingly long awaited order "Fire!", quickly followed by "Down to thirty feet!"

As the submarine slid downwards all on board heard the dull thud of the explosion—the 'tin fish' had found its mark. Another peep with the periscope showed the Turk settling by the stern, but it also revealed the fact that swarms of patrol boats were rushing towards the British submarine, whose position had been shown up by the line of bubbles from the speeding torpedo.

There was only one thing to do. Lieutenant Holbrook gave the order to dive and, a few minutes later, B-11 was resting on the bottom while the surface of the water above was lashed into foam by shells and propellers. Below they could hear the noise of the patrol boats' progress and the sounds continued without ceasing.

B-11 then considered the problem of getting home. It was a problem : the submarine was worse than blind. Her Skipper knew they were somewhere between Kephez and "The Narrows," but exactly where he did not know. Added to that, the lenses of the spirit compasses were fogged and consequently useless. He realised that something would have to be done quickly. He was not worrying about the busy patrol boats—they were comparatively harmless while he kept deeply submerged—but the air in the submarine would not last many more hours : it was already getting " thick."

The idea of rising to the surface for bearings could not be considered. The first show of the periscope above the surface would have resulted in a tornado of shells, so Lieutenant Holbrook ordered full speed ahead and steered in the direction he imagined was the way home. Time after time B-11 bumped heavily on the bottom, but her Skipper had to risk opening up her plates and carry on.

Judging at length that he was under and past the minefield again *if* he had guessed the direction correctly, Lieutenant Holbrook brought the submarine up to twenty feet and ordered the periscope to be raised.

Only a few moments were necessary for him to see there was land on his port beam and fix his position by landmarks. He was on the right track, but he was forced to dive again : the shore batteries were less than a mile apart and B-11 was compelled to remain submerged until Hellas was astern on the way out. Then, to the relief of all hands, she was brought to the surface and " ventilated." She had been submerged for nine hours, which was about the limit for a B class submarine, and the air in her was absolutely foul and near the danger point.

For his courage and daring in taking the first British submarine into those narrow waters, sinking the Turkish battleship and bringing back valuable information that enabled other submarines to repeat the operation, Lieutenant Holbrook received the Victoria Cross, his Second-in-Command, Lieutenant S. T. Winn, the D.S.O., and the rest of the crew were decorated.

JOHN F. C. WESTERMAN.

THE BREAKER OF ROCKS

Past Cannibals and Cataracts with Stanley.

THIN, sallow and hollow-cheeked, yet strong of voice and firm of bearing, a white man stood just sixty years ago upon the shore of a great Central African river. He was surrounded by a motley crowd of dark-skinned humanity—Arabs, Zanzibaris, Negroes, men, women and children—to most of whom his word was law. They called him the Breaker of Rocks; for no obstacle could daunt, no illness deter, or danger frighten him. This man was Henry M. Stanley. Successively workhouse boy, ship's lad, soldier, sailor, war correspondent, explorer, he was now leader of an expedition to cross the heart of unknown Africa.

He looked down at the river from Nyangwe, a lonely outpost of Arab slavers and ivory traders, far to the west of Lake Tanganyika. It was surrounded on land by cannibals, by death-dealing snakes, by wild elephants and lions; over the water lurked malarial mosquitoes and tsetse flies; within the water were hippopotami of vast bulk and uncertain temper. Death in a score of forms confronted the traveller in this delusively beautiful country. Yet Stanley must travel both on land and by water for something like 2,000 miles if he were to attain his object of tracing the river's course to the Atlantic Ocean.

The river itself—brown, deep, silent, and nearly a mile wide—was a mystery of the first order. It was called the Lualaba; and more than one explorer had imagined that it described an immense curve in the heart of Africa and became the Congo, which at that time was only known for a few miles from the ocean. But although the famous travellers Livingstone and Cameron had both stood at this place before Stanley, and had both desired to float down the mysterious river, lack of canoes had prevented them. Livingstone was now dead; and Stanley, his friend and admirer, had come to complete his work. Stanley had brought out a special boat, built in five sections, from England; she was the *Lady Alice*, forty feet long, and had already carried him safely through many a storm on the great African lakes; while her crew, headed by the brave coxswain Uledi, would have followed their leader to the death, and had proved their worth in many a stern tussle. Stanley's total following, however, numbered one hundred and fifty-four, the majority of whom were kept in obedience only by the sheer terror of his name ; and to provide them with boats was a task beyond even Stanley's power at the moment. He therefore proposed to cross the Lualaba, push through the forest beyond, and at some friendly native village downstream to purchase or build the necessary dug-outs ; with this equipment he would then follow the stream to its mouth or his own destruction. Owing to the arrant cowardice of his people, he had lately engaged Tippoo Tib, an Arab slaver of evil repute, with three hundred followers, to convoy him for sixty marches through the forest whose green border could be seen across the stream ; while he himself and his sole remaining white companion, Frank Pocock, a young Kentishman, distributed amongst his own people the fifty muskets and Snyder rifles of the expedition. For, unlike most African explorers, Stanley had come with the intention of going whither he chose, and of fighting his way through, should that prove necessary ; and when it is remembered that a strong Arab party had been almost destroyed by the dwarfs of the Congo forest quite recently, and that Stanley himself achieved success only after thirty-two pitched battles, we see that his decision was a wise one. It is characteristic of Stanley that before leaving Nyangwe they tossed pennies to decide whether they should go up the Lualaba (the easier course) or down towards the unknown; and although the coin indicated the safer route every time, he elected to take the dangerous one !

Headed by the Arabs, the long file of heavily-laden and chattering carriers crossed the Lualaba and began to wind away towards the forest beyond. From its verge this forest looked invitingly cool and green, despite the vast tangle of thorny undergrowth ; but from within it was soon seen to be a dismal, silent, dripping wilderness, with sticky clay and rivulets underfoot and only the dimmest of greenish light overhead ; ropy lianas hung from the branches like cables ; the air resembled that of a stuffy hothouse ; spiny plants tore the travellers' skins ; hosts of venomous little ants bit them, and roots and tangles were as if by malice aforethought constantly tripping them up. The men began to curse, and then to grumble. The heavy sections of the boat caught upon every obstacle. The marches grew shorter and shorter. The Arab escort was as much afraid as were the people it was supposed to guard. Tippoo Tib asked to be released from his bargain. Finally, Stanley himself in desperation altered his course so as to reach the river's brink ; and while he, with the crew of the *Lady Alice* and a few canoes, descended the stream, the main party, under Tippoo Tib, followed along the bank, or as near to the bank as that dreadful forest would permit.

[*Keystone.*

Typical swamp and jungle land. The natives have killed a young hippopotamus.

Now, however, their troubles speedily multiplied ; for villages were thickly clustered along the river ; and the hostile inhabitants, scenting in the intruders an excellent item for tomorrow's dinner, rushed out to battle, with tom-toms beating and war-horns blowing, in a state of frenzied excitement that only seemed to increase the farther Stanley's people advanced. The villages comprised each a

"The men began to curse and then to grumble."

long street of grass huts, fronted on each side by a row of grinning and bleached human skulls, which were sunk into the earth like a kerb; the rubbish heaps contained limb bones, pieces of flesh and other relics of the savages' unholy feasts. To argue with such people was a waste of words, or at least so Stanley thought; poisoned darts and razor-edged spears could only be countered by bullets.

Matters soon came to a crisis, for Stanley and his little party, who had got too far ahead of the land force, were surrounded both by land and water, the savages outnumbering them by twenty to one. Nothing dismayed, he ordered his boats to be drawn up at a clearing, and he and his followers, three dozen in all, took possession of the deserted village; an act which aroused the natives to a pitch of unusual hate. Orders were given to close up the ends of the street with a strong fence of thorn bushes; the ground was cleared for fifty yards from the houses on either side; marksmen were placed in the nearest trees, and others in the houses; and in this wise Stanley calmly awaited the enemy's onset. "Prepare, prepare! They're coming!" yelled someone; and as he spoke, the savages rushed to the edge of the clearing in hundreds, hurled their heavy spears through the thorn hedge, shot their arrows over it, and raised a terrifying and unearthly din, with shrieks, war-cries and beating of drums. Stanley and his men replied less noisily but with far greater effect ; yet, although most of the shots went home, the savages maintained the attack for two whole hours. Then darkness came, but it brought no relief ; for from the bushes arrows were rained upon the defenders all night. So tired were his men that Stanley had to have cold water poured upon some of them to keep them awake.

Morning came at last, bringing a fresh danger ; for the enemy's fleet of powerful dug-out canoes, with from five hundred to eight hundred warriors aboard, now got ready to descend upon the place.

" The savages rushed to the edge of the clearing."

Each canoe carried from twenty to thirty oarsmen, who drove her through the water in magnificent style; while in the prow stood fighting men, spear in hand; the drums beat incessantly and everything portended a combined attack upon the little party by land and water.

At that instant a shout was heard from the forest. The attack paused; and then, to Stanley's intense relief, the head of his land force emerged. But the enemy were so numerous, and by beat of drum had rallied round them so many neighbours from the adjacent villages, that the whole party of the explorers, including Tippoo and his men, were forced into the village, there to abide the issue. Night came again, with the fight still undecided; and Stanley determined to cut off the enemy's fleet, which had retired to an island in mid-stream. While the warriors slept or boasted round their camp fires, Stanley and a few picked men stole upon them with muffled oars, cut away thirty-six fine canoes, and let them float downstream to the tip of the island, where Pocock was waiting to secure them. By this means the party were able to get away. Tippoo Tib, however, now thoroughly frightened, asked again to go back; so Stanley released him; and taking his own people on in the captured fleet, the intrepid explorer led them down the river, to the cry of "Forward! Victory or death!"

News of an enemy spreads through the forest like a shaft of light. Soon Stanley had to fight again, and yet again, merely for the privilege of passing by: and it was only at rare intervals that food could be procured for the many mouths that depended on him. The canoes of the cannibals always outnumbered his, and for the most part were larger and better manned. Once they swept down upon the *Lady Alice*, their people drumming, shouting and gesticulating with the cheerful refrain, "Meat, meat! Ah ha! We shall have plenty of meat! Bo, bo, bo, bo, bo-o-o!" After a taste of bullets and slugs, however, they decided that the "meat" had better be allowed to escape. On another occasion sixty-three huge canoes, filled with the bravest warriors, lay in wait for the explorers at the mouth of the great river Aruwimi; but despite the immense difference in numbers, the result was never in doubt. These implacable enemies were succeeded by more timid tribes, who needed much tact and coaxing before they would turn from sullen suspicion into interested friendship; and with these people many a bond of blood-brotherhood had to be made—a disgusting ceremony, one man of each party making a cut in the other's arm and then sucking the blood from the wound.

Meanwhile, the river, which had led north and north for so long that even Stanley began to wonder where it would end, suddenly turned west, next to point straight towards the mouth of the Congo.

" Once Pocock ordered a canoe to take him down another cascade, only for the canoe to be lost and his own body swept away."

It was several miles wide, was crowded with islands, and the way was barred by rapid after rapid, each seemingly worse than the last. In these places the water raged and spumed so furiously that often no canoe could live there ; and the heavy craft had to be man-hauled alongshore, constantly dragging against the rattan canes that were improvised into ropes. Once the *Lady Alice* shot over a rapid with Stanley on board ; the din of the rushing water was so great that the coxswain could only steer by watching the motion of Stanley's hand ;

and yet by a miracle they escaped disaster. Once Pocock ordered a canoe to take him down another cascade, only for the canoe to be lost and his own corpse swept away by the irresistible current. The people became despondent ; their leader went grey with anxiety ; nevertheless, he tore down all obstacles, once even hauling his great dug-outs over a hill higher than St. Paul's Cathedral. But many of his boats and some of his best and most faithful followers were lost in the process. One rescue was particularly exciting ; it occurred at the second of the seven cataracts which form Stanley Falls.

One of the chiefs, named Zaidi, was upset out of a canoe, and was borne with the wreck to the very lip of the fall, where the wood fortunately jammed, holding him up with his back to the boiling waves below. A rope was hastily made of canes, and a canoe, tied to it, was sent down towards him ; but after several attempts the rope broke and the craft swept past him and was torn to fragments in the great whirlpool beyond. Stanley then tried lashing a canoe with ropes fore and aft, besides a third amidships ; and in this his fearless coxswain, Uledi, ventured with one native boy towards the drowning man. Five times did they reach the edge of the drop without getting near him ; the sixth time they came within ten yards, and Uledi threw him a rope ; but scarcely had he grasped it when the cables snapped and Uledi and the boy were hurled overboard. The position now, however, was reversed, for Zaidi served as an anchor to keep them back ; and after a desperate struggle all three clambered on to a rocky islet which overhung the fall. There, dripping and exhausted, they had to stop all night ; but next day Stanley and his people hauled them back to safety.

This famous journey, so packed with thrills, ended at last with the complete accomplishment of what Stanley had set himself to do. But when he neared Boma, the first white settlement, his people were demoralised by scurvy, worn down with hunger, and could scarcely drag themselves along. So he sent on Uledi and one or two others, bearing a famous message : " To any gentleman who speaks English. I have arrived at this place from Zanzibar with one hundred and fifteen souls, men, women and children, in a state of imminent starvation." Some English and Portuguese traders received it ; and very soon after that the heroic Stanley and his people were enjoying the luxuries of civilisation.

B. WEBSTER SMITH.

[*Wide World Photos.*

WAITING TO BE PICKED UP.

This pilot has deliberately crashed his plane into the sea while a film was being shot.

CRASHING PLANES FOR A LIVING

YOU are holding your breath. Your fingers are digging tightly into the arms of your seat. Both feet are pressed hard on the floor and you are rigid with excitement as you watch the thrilling drama on the cinema screen.

Two aeroplanes are battling in the sky. Then one of them dives. It plunges earthwards with a shrill whine. It is out of control. The pilot is struggling desperately in the cockpit. But it is too late. There is a crash. The doomed machine plunges its propeller boss into the ground. With a grinding, a crackling and a crunching the tail swings into the air, and the fuselage crumples.

The scene fades. Around you, people are gasping. It is then that someone behind you, one of those people who claims to know exactly how everything is done, says in a loud and bored voice:

"Of course, it's all a fake. They do these things with little models."

He is quite wrong. There is nothing faked about aeroplane crashes in films. The nerve-tingling wrecks which you see are real wrecks.

The man who holds the record for having crashed the largest number of planes for the films is Dick Grace; he has brought the job to a fine art. At one time Grace worked for a firm of tyre manufacturers. His work was to test the tyres, and he did it by fitting the tyres to an old car, which he drove at top speed into a brick wall. He had a nack of doing this without hurting himself and so, naturally enough, when film producers were in need of a man to carry out some particularly dangerous stunt, they sought him out.

When Grace began, he undertook all manner of reckless scenes. But after a time he decided to specialise in aeroplane crashes.

"It can't last for ever," people used to say. "One day Grace's luck will give out, and then he'll break his neck."

But Grace was not foolhardy enough to rely on luck. He studied the construction of various types of machines. He pored over blue prints and mathematical formulas. He tried to work out, in theory, just what would happen to the machines when they hit the ground at different angles and at varying speeds. He became so skilled in his work that he could crash a machine in any fashion that the film directors asked for. He could land right way up, and smash the undercarriage; he could crash on one wing; he could turn a wrecked plane upside down. He even managed a crash in which the plane hit the ground nose first, flipped its tail in the air, wobbled a little as if it was about to go over on its back, and then remained balanced on its nose, sticking straight up into the air.

On another occasion he was shown a yellow ring, ten feet in diameter, that had been painted on the ground, and was asked if he could turn a plane over on its back somewhere near the ring. He took a handkerchief from his pocket, and spread it on the ground.

"I'll do better than that," he said. "I'll land so that this handkerchief is under the wreck."

He took the machine into the air, hurled it at the yellow ring, crashed, and turned the plane right over. As he was hanging head downwards in the cockpit, suspended by his safety strap, he reached down and gathered up the handkerchief, which was right underneath him.

One day Dick Grace was asked to crash a Fokker D7 of the type used in the Great War. For the scene in which he was to play he was asked to take off, climb to a height of seventy feet, when he was supposed to be attacked by another machine which would cause him

[*Keystone.*

A SPECTACULAR CRASH.

With a grinding, a crackling and a crunching, the tail swings into the air and the fuselage crumples.

to dive and crash. On the day appointed for the stunt the sky was a cloudless blue. The scene called for clouds in the sky, and the work was postponed. On the following day the sky was still cloudless. Four more days came and went. Not a cloud appeared. An attempt was made to fake clouds with smoke, but this failed.

This continual, irritating postponement got on Grace's nerves. He was anxious to get the job over. The long wait imposed a powerful mental strain. He began to feel that the stunt was fated. Another week wore on. Still no clouds, and Grace began to suffer from sleeplessness through brooding over his coming ordeal. Three weeks passed before a cloudy day dawned. Grace hurried to the field where the scene was to be shot.

"Are you feeling all right, Dick ?" asked the director anxiously.

"Never better in my life," declared the stunt man stoutly.

"Don't say that if you don't mean it. We can wait another day or two if you like."

"No more waiting, thanks ! Let's get this job over."

Grace superintended the arrangements for the stunt.

The wing struts of the Fokker D7 were sawn partly through so that they would crumple on the impact, and lessen the shock. The motor was warmed up, then the fuel tank was drained until only about a gallon of petrol was left. This was done to lessen the danger of fire when the machine crashed.

Grace had his own squad of rescue men standing by. They were equipped with fire-extinguishers, hack-saws, axes and pliers. A first aid unit and an ambulance also stood ready. Every man in the squad had been thoroughly trained so that he would know what to do in an emergency, but before entering his Fokker, Grace gave instructions that, even if he appeared to be hurt, no one was to approach the machine until the cameramen had exposed as much film as they required. There could be only one excuse for ignoring these orders, and that was if fire broke out.

Grace settled into the cockpit, and strapped himself in with his safety belts. He switched the engine on. A mechanic swung the propeller, and the engine spluttered with a series of explosions. He opened the throttle and the engine settled into a steady roar. The machine that was to pretend to shoot Grace down took off and climbed into the sky, coming back overhead with a vertical banking turn.

Grace took a last look round. He made a careful note of the spot where he was to crash, judged the distance to the spot where the cameramen stood, and then signalled that he was ready to take off. The Fokker, being an old machine, had no kind of wheel or air brakes. It was held by chocks under the wheels. When these were removed, the Fokker taxied forward until it picked up air speed.

Grace took off. The Fokker slanted into the air.

Down came the attacking machine. Grace pushed his control stick forward. The Fokker thrust its nose towards the ground. A quick glance at the air-speed indicator showed the stunter that he was doing a hundred and ten miles an hour. He had never crashed at such a speed before. It was dangerously fast.

But he was not frightened. All his mind was concentrated on giving the cameramen a thrilling scene. He found a fleeting moment to marvel at their pluck. After all, it needed an iron nerve to stand behind a camera while an aeroplane was pitched at you at a speed of a hundred and ten miles an hour. The slightest error on the part of the pilot would mean death for the cameramen.

[*Topical.*

An air crash staged for the films.

Grace tensed for the coming impact.

The sky reeled, and vanished behind him. A spread of green earth filled his vision, and a yellow circle on the ground jumped to meet him. He moved the rudder bar slightly. The plane swayed, and dragged one wing-tip into the ground.

This was the crash!

Grace tore off his goggles and threw them away. He cut his switch, closed the throttle, and turned off the petrol.

The wing crumpled. The plane heeled round. The propeller dug into the ground and dissolved in a shower of flying splinters. Grace ducked lower into the cockpit and held his breath. So far everything was going well. The crash was happening just as he had calculated it.

Then an unforeseen disaster happened.

He had calculated that the force of the impact would smash the undercarriage. He was wrong. It held together in spite of the crash and bounced the plane into the air.

The plane tilted and the undamaged wing, catching the wind, swept the Fokker into the air once more. Grace realised that unless he acted swiftly the wrecked machine would be swept among the cameras! There was only one thing to do. He realised that he might kill himself, but he did it. He pushed the stick forward as far as it would go. The Fokker came down with a crash on its nose.

The cameramen stuck to their posts, in spite of the fact that it looked as if the tangled aeroplane was going to fall on top of them. Their lives were in Grace's hands, and they trusted him. The noise of the impact was nerve-wracking. The machine smashed itself to matchwood. Grace did not move.

As soon as the cameras ceased turning, the rescue team rushed to the wreck. Grace's safety belt had broken. He had been flung forward, and his head had gone clean through the instrument board in the cockpit.

When they got him out they discovered that his neck was broken, but he was still alive. They rushed him to hospital. Medical science was called in to save this prince of stunters. He did not die.

Within a few months he was out and about again, back at the old job, crashing planes once more. The words of the wiseacres had come true. Grace had broken his neck, but even that did not stop him, for since that day he has wrecked dozens more planes to give cinema-goers a thrill.

STUART CHESMORE.

[*Wide World Photos*

A British 'Ace' cornering with his wing-tip scraping the ground.

A THRILL ON THE 'PICTURES': DESCENDING BY PARACHUTE FROM A BURNING PASSENGER LINER.

"BRAVING A VERITABLE BARRAGE OF FIRE FROM THE GROUND, MILLS LET GO ALL HIS BOMBS AT ONCE."

THE ZEPPELIN FIGHTER

The Epic Story of Flight Sub-Lieutenant Warneford, V.C.

IN the glorious history of the British air services during the Great War there is no more stirring chapter than that which records the gallant deeds of the Zeppelin Fighters — that small band of determined airmen who, by dint of unparalleled bravery and devotion to duty, freed our skies from the grim menace of the Terror that Flew by Night.

Riding the night skies high above a darkened countryside they hunted their mammoth quarry among the clouds, guided by the questing fingers of searchlights and the flaming bursts of anti-aircraft gunfire. Then, the raider located, a red Verey light would flare out in signal to the gunners to cease fire and down would plunge the Zeppelin Fighter to pit his frail craft single-handed against the massed guns of the giant airship and its deadly cargo of high explosive.

It was work that called for brave men with nerves of steel and, as ever in Britain's history, such men were forthcoming in our time of need. Before the Terror was ended, the names of many heroes were to be inscribed upon the roll of fame of England's Zeppelin Fighters, and, at the head of that list, was to be the name of a nineteen-year old boy, Flight Sub-Lieutenant R. A. J. Warneford, R.N.A.S., the single-handed destroyer of the first Zeppelin to be brought down by an aeroplane.

Born at Darjeeling, Bengal, Reginald Alexander John Warneford came to England as a child to be educated at the Grammar School at Stratford-on-Avon. His school career, however, was brief, for the young Warneford had heard the call of the sea and, so insistent were his demands for a sailor's life, that, before he was fourteen he had joined the Mercantile Marine as an apprentice and was outward bound on his first voyage.

The outbreak of war found him a fully-fledged ship's officer eagerly waiting for the end of a long voyage so that he could do his bit before the War was over. At last his ship docked in England and a few days later, in February, 1915, Warneford had joined the Royal Naval Air Service with the rank of Sub-Lieutenant. His knowledge of seamanship and navigation stood him in good stead in the new service and, proving an apt pupil in the handling of an aeroplane, he soon qualified as a pilot and, as a Flight Sub-Lieutenant, was posted to the R.N.A.S. station at Dunkirk.

His first encounter with the giant raiders that were destined to make his name immortal occurred within a few weeks of his arrival at Dunkirk. The date was May the 17th, 1915, and in the early hours of that morning three Zeppelins, L.Z. 37, 38 and 39, were sighted off Dunkirk on their way back from a raid on England. It was the first opportunity that the naval pilots had yet had of getting to grips with their enemy in the air and they were not slow to take advantage of the chance. Within a few moments of sighting the raiders, nine machines had taken-off from Dunkirk to intercept them, and leading the attackers were Sub-Lieutenant Warneford and Squadron-Commander Spencer Grey. With his engine roaring all-out, Warneford climbed to the attack, overhauled the huge bulk of L.Z. 39 and opened fire at close quarters. But the Zeppelin commander was ready for him and at the first sound of gunfire, he jettisoned several tons of water-ballast so that the lightened airship suddenly shot up out of range and was soon flying in safety at a far greater height than Warneford's heavily-loaded machine could reach. Reluctantly he was obliged to give up the chase and return to Dunkirk, not at all consoled by the distinction of having made the first aerial attack upon a Zeppelin, and determined that his next encounter with the enemy would be attended by a very different result.

Actually, the L.Z. 39 did not escape altogether unscathed, for, over Ostend, she came lower to discover her position and was pounced upon by another R.N.A.S. pilot, Flight-Commander A. W. Bigsworth, who swooped to within twenty feet of her back and dropped four bombs. The bombs did not succeed in setting her on fire and, once again, she eluded her attacker by dropping water-ballast and rising out of range. It was later learned, however, that she had been severely damaged, and that an officer and five men had been seriously wounded by the explosions from Bigsworth's bombs—the first casualties inflicted on the Zeppelin service by British pilots.

Several weeks passed before the Dunkirk pilots had a second chance of trying conclusions with the raiders and, meanwhile, their determination to strike a decisive blow had been strengthened by a taunting message which the Zeppelin commander, Linnarz, had dropped on his way home from carrying out the first raid on London on the night of May the 31st. The message, written on a card in Linnarz's own handwriting, was addressed to the defence force and read:

"*You English! We have come and will come again soon to kill or cure! German!*"

The R.N.A.S. pilots at Dunkirk knew that Linnarz's head-quarters, and the main base for Zeppelins raiding England, was at Evere, and it was decided that it was high time a call was paid upon the boastful airship commander. There was much keen rivalry for the honour of taking part in this "courtesy call," but finally it was limited to Lieutenant J. P. Wilson and Sub-Lieutenant J. S. Mills, who were to attack Evere, while Sub-Lieutenant Warneford and another pilot were to provide a diversion by launching a simultaneous attack upon the companion airship base at Bercham St. Agathe.

[*L.E.A.*

Flight Sub-Lieutenant Warneford, V.C.

On the night of June the 7th, the four machines took-off and while Warneford and his companion laid a course for Bercham St. Agathe, Wilson and Mills flew towards Evere. Reaching the airship base

By courtesy of] [*United Artists.*

A Zeppelin returning from a raid.

without detection, Wilson dropped three sixty-five pound bombs, which sent up dense smoke but no flames. Then Mills took a hand in the game and, braving a veritable barrage of fire from the ground, let go all his bombs together and was rewarded an instant later by a terrific explosion that marked the end of L.Z. 38 and its shed.

Meanwhile, Warneford had been gallantly fighting his way alone towards his objective through a heavy mist, his companion, by the failure of his instruments, having been forced to land soon after starting. Warneford was almost despairing of finding Bercham St. Agathe, when suddenly out of the mist there loomed a huge grey shape, coming steadily towards him. Banking sharply, he put his machine into a steep turn, narrowly missing a head-on collision with one of the very airships he was on his way to destroy! Recovering from the shock of his narrow escape, he saw that by an amazing stroke of luck he had caught the L.Z. 37 returning from a raid. The Zeppelin's crew did not appear to have sighted him and, fearful of losing his quarry in the thickening mist, Warneford decided to stalk the airship until a clear patch was reached.

Over Bruges the mist dispersed and Warneford launched his attack upon the raider, only to be met with such a devastating hail of fire from the gondola guns that he was forced to dive out of range while he manœuvred for a new position from which to attack. But the Zeppelin commander was not easily to be robbed of his prey and actually turned after him, keeping the machine under a steady rain of bullets. Height was Warneford's only hope of making a successful attack and for several precious minutes he forced his Morane higher and higher, until at a height of eleven thousand feet he nosed over and went hurtling down upon his quarry. Straight into a hail of fire from the airship's roof-gun he dived and held his dive unfalteringly until he was less than a hundred feet above the broad grey back of the dirigible. Then he straightened out, jerked his bomb-releases, and planted all six of his twenty-pound bombs fairly and squarely along the Zeppelin's length.

By courtesy of] [*United Artists.*

Machine-gunners in action on top of a Zeppelin.

There was a blinding flash, a terrific roar of exploding gas and bombs, and the great bulk of L.Z. 37 dissolved in an inferno of flames. But so determined had Warneford been to make sure of his enemy's destruction that he had taken no heed of his own danger, and the first warning he had of his peril was when his machine, caught by the terrific concussion of the exploding airship, was hurled bodily upwards for two hundred feet and turned upside down. Only his shoulder-straps saved him from being thrown out, and when he at last succeeded in righting the machine, it was to find that his engine had stopped and that he was faced with the necessity of making a forced landing in the semi-darkness some thirty miles inside the enemy's territory!

He chose a field close by a wood, managed, by superb skill, to land his machine safely and at once set about destroying it so that it should not fall into enemy hands. A flaming match was already poised to throw into the petrol-tank when the daring idea came to him to try to repair the machine and escape. The damage, he discovered, was due to a petrol joint that had been fractured by the force of the explosion, and working stealthily but quickly, he succeeded in repairing it in just over thirty minutes of nerve-racking toil. The job done, he restarted his engine and just managed to scramble into the cockpit of the already moving Morane as a patrol of enemy cavalry came galloping up.

By this time the mist had gathered again, and once in the air Warneford was quickly lost. He flew on until his fuel was exhausted and then, for a second time in that eventful night, made a successful forced landing—this time to find himself at Cape Gris Nez and the hero of the hour.

For his gallant achievement, the first victory over a Zeppelin in the air, the young Sub-Lieutenant received the Victoria Cross from the hands of the King himself, while a grateful France awarded him the Croix de Guerre. But fate decreed that he should not long survive to enjoy the honours that he had so bravely won, and ten days after his heroic victory the twenty-one-year-old hero was killed when a machine that he was testing near Paris broke up in mid-air.

So passed Warneford, first of the Zeppelin Fighters, whose name will ever live while men remember the valorous deeds of Britain's Warriors of the Sky.

T. STANHOPE SPRIGG.

"THERE WAS A BLINDING FLASH AND A TERRIFIC ROAR OF EXPLODING GAS."

"HE FLEW ON UNTIL HIS FUEL WAS EXHAUSTED."

THE MAN ON THE ISLAND

The Adventures of Alexander Selkirk.

THE Thames watermen and the London 'prentices must have been greatly excited on the 14th of October in the year 1711. An English ship, called *The Duke,* had sailed up the river on the early tide, and about eleven o'clock in the morning, she dropped anchor just below Old London Bridge.

The Duke was a famous buccaneer just home from a three years' voyage. And Dampier, the great English seaman and privateer, was her master-pilot. Privateering was reckoned an honourable profession in those days. It seemed to make little difference whether England was at war or at peace with other nations. And on the Spanish Main, the Pacific Ocean or the China Seas, every ship that didn't fly the English flag was reckoned fair game.

The Duke had come home laden with treasure, ingots of gold and silver, pieces of eight, and much valuable plate. During her long voyage she had fought more than a score of battles, and had captured many rich prizes. Very quickly the news spread from London Bridge to Temple Bar that Dampier was "home again" with his ship full of Spanish treasure.

It wasn't the treasure which half-filled the buccaneer which made the arrival of the ship such an historic occasion, however. Dampier and his companions, more than two years previously, had found a long-lost, marooned sailor living alone, on the island of Juan de Fernandez in the Pacific Ocean, nearly four hundred miles from the mainland of Chili.

This man's name was Alexander Selkirk . . . the real *Robinson Crusoe*. And after being marooned, he had lived alone on the island for four years and four months. This was the real treasure which Dampier's little ship brought home. And had this mariner not been rescued and brought back to England, the greatest story in the English language would never have been written.

The book has been translated into more than forty languages. And it is one of the half-dozen books written by Englishmen which have helped to make our country loved by the foreigner. A little while ago a Hungarian said to an English Scoutmaster: "We love you English people because you gave us Robinson."

Alexander Selkirk was the son of a cobbler. He was born in the little fishing village of Largo, on the Fifeshire coast in the year 1676. "Luckie laddie," his mother called him, because he happened to be the seventh son. If it's "lucky" to become famous she was right. But there's bad luck and good luck, and the cobbler's son sampled both varieties early in life. His father tried very hard to make Young Alec a cobbler. But from his earliest boyhood the tang of the salt spray was in the lad's blood. He couldn't abide the idea of being a stay-at-home, hammering all day at the last.

When he was in his teens, a curious thing happened to Young Selkirk. One Sunday morning in kirk, during a long sermon, he happened to commit the serious crime of laughing aloud. And in those days, when the kirk rule was so powerful across the border, this was a very real offence. Next morning a notice was affixed to the shoemaker's door summoning Alexander Selkirk, son of John Selkirk, Shoemaker, to appear before the elders of the kirk. Young Alec didn't stay in Largo to face the music. That very day he ran away to sea, found a ship, and by midnight the Fifeshire coast had been left behind. It was the beginning of a great adventure that was to thrill the whole world. Before long, the cobbler's son was sailing with the pirates on the Spanish Main, the Indian Ocean, and the South Sea. Piracy, filibustering, and buccaneering were rife then.

In his many voyages Young Selkirk, who soon became a sailing master, trod the deck with such renowned seamen as Woodes Rogers,

Stradling, and Dampier. It was a thrilling if a lawless life looking out for Spanish galleons, Dutch Indiamen, and carracks coming home deep-laden with treasure from the Isthmus, rounding the Horn from far-away Cathay, fighting almost every ship they met, and raiding the new settlements along the South American coast.

But after a while Selkirk grew tired of the life, and the quarrelsome spirit of his partners. He began to reflect a good deal, then to read the Bible that had lain so long at the bottom of his sea-chest. Perhaps he also remembered some of the minister's long sermons he had heard years ago at the kirk. Besides, about this time he had a curious dream. He foresaw in a dream the wreck of the ship in which he was now sailing. This was the *Cinque Ports*. Years afterwards Selkirk accidentally heard how this dream came true. The *Cinque Ports* was wrecked, and Stradling with his crew became Spanish prisoners, and were very ill-treated.

Some time before the wreck, however, the *Cinque Ports* had put into the lonely island of Juan de Fernandez to get fresh water. Just before they left, Selkirk approached his captain and begged to be left behind. Stradling was furious at first. He would not agree to maroon his sailing-master, for there were few navigators at that time who knew those distant seas. But Selkirk, whose mood had been strange for days past, was resolved.

"Do you mean, Selkirk, that you want to be left behind on that uninhabited island?" asked Stradling.

"I do, Captain. I am tired of being a pirate."

At length the captain agreed. A boat was lowered, and Selkirk was landed on the shore with his sea-chest containing a few clothes, a gun, flint and steel, a pound of gun-powder, a knife, a hatchet . . . and his Bible. As the ship sailed away the marooned seaman danced about his few possessions, and sang for sheer joy. But as evening fell and he cast a farewell look at his old ship, now hull down, with only her tops'ls showing above the darkening horizon, he realised too late his tragic situation.

It was worse still when the curtain of night fell about him. The strange noises on the island terrified him. The power of sleep forsook him. All that night he sat upon his sea-chest on the beach half mad with fear. When dawn came this phase passed. Hunger asserted itself, and for a while he became reconciled to his condition.

He lived at first upon wild fruits, parsnips, water-cresses, cabbage palms, and a few fish caught close inshore. One day he shot a wild goat, dressed it, then lit a fire with his flint and steel, cooked the goat's flesh, and had a great feast. Then he built a rude hut, to protect himself from the wind and rain, next he made himself a table and a chair. Using his little powder sparingly, he began to hunt the wild goats afoot. He caught a few young kids and domesticated them. He found a few oats growing wild. He cultivated them carefully, and made a rough, coarse bread. The first oats had probably been shaken out of some canvas bag by an earlier visitor. One morning he caught a crawfish weighing eight or nine pounds.

The rats began to worry him dreadfully. They gnawed him while he slept. But one day another castaway came to his camp. It wasn't Man Friday . . . he never came. It was a ship's cat, and its friendly purr was the nearest approach to human speech the castaway was to hear for four years and four months. Felix seemed as pleased to see Selkirk as the marooned mariner was to encounter Felix. They became great pals. The cat never left Selkirk. It was the rats that left him from now onward.

Selkirk was so busy now with his hands, that for a while time passed pleasantly. He made himself a cap, jacket and breeches of goatskin. He found iron hoops on the beach, and fashioned them into tools, making handles of horn. He found a nail in the sand, and fashioned it into a needle. He used thin strips of dried goatskin for thread to sew his clothes. He had no shoes and went bare-foot. His powder had run out now. Stradling had only left him a pound. He had become so fleet of foot, however, that he could sometimes overtake the wild goats, leaping with amazing agility from one crag to another.

One day, however, he missed his footing just as he gripped the horns of a huge goat. Beast and man fell together down a chasm. Three days and three nights Selkirk lay unconscious on the dead goat. He told the time on this occasion by the growth of the moon. He kept his calendar most religiously by carving a notch on a hardwood tree, from first landing in October, 1704 till his departure in February, 1709, though it wore his knife to a thin strip. But having been a mariner since his youth, the practice of keeping a daily log had become a habit. He used no salt for seasoning his food, but he flavoured it with the ground wood of the pimento tree (Jamaica pepper).

"HE BUILT HIMSELF A RUDE HUT."

After a while there came periods of great depression to the marooned seaman. He began to read his Bible daily. Weeks and months had passed, and he became haunted with the fear that he would be left to die on his uninhabited island, ten thousand miles from his native village. He resolved to build a huge beacon of logs and brushwood on a hill-top over-looking the wide and lonely Pacific. Then, every day from morning till night, he began to scan the horizon more eagerly, so that, if any ship should show her tops'ls above the far horizon, he might light a great bonfire quickly as a signal of distress.

The first year passed away and never a sail hove in sight. The second year passed, and the third year was nearly ended, when Selkirk saw, or fancied he saw, the upper sails of a ship hull down to the eastward. He raced to the hill-top, his heart beating wildly with a frantic hope. Striking his steel on the flint he sent a shower of sparks on to the dried punk at the base of the pile, and a little flame shot up. The next moment the huge beacon was alight.

The marooned exile, breathless with exertion, then turned to look seaward, shading his eyes from the climbing sun.

Poor Selkirk. No answering signal came across the water. The tops'ls of the distant vessel gradually faded out into the faint mist of the far-flung horizon. And, inconsolable, the exile, as evening fell, went down to his rude shelter.

Four years and four months passed away, then one exciting afternoon, as dusk began to fall, on the 31st of January, 1709, two ships rounded the headland to south-eastward, and came almost suddenly into view. As good fortune would have it, they were English ships, the *Duke* and *Duchess* out of Bristol. Probably they were named after the Duke of Marlborough and his Lady, who, at that time, were very powerful at the English court. Darkness fell, but Selkirk's beacon was blazing merrily all that night, and both ships had anchored off the island, after replying to the land signal.

Next morning at dawn the *Duke* lowered a boat. Dampier remained on board, but the master, Captain Dover, Mr. Fry and six armed men came riding through the surf, expecting a brush with Spaniards. There was only one man waiting for them on the beach. It was Selkirk. He was gesticulating wildly, waving his arms and showing them where to land.

" He is a wild man," said Mr. Fry. " He is dressed in goatskins, but he is carrying an old flint-lock musket. Stand ready . . ! "

Selkirk, having heard no human speech for so many years, seemed unable to talk. But he rushed forward, threw down his musket, and embraced the first man who landed.

The marooned exile, who jabbered somewhat incoherently, was taken back to the ship.

It was Dampier himself who first recognised the long-lost Englishman. "God, if it isn't Selkirk . . . my old shipmate, Selkirk!" exclaimed the master-pilot.

"*Ye-es—Sel-kirk—!*" stammered the exile, in deep, slow, uncertain tones. Gradually his speech returned. And a little later, bit by bit, he told his strange story to the buccaneers. But to hear once again the sound of human speech, in his own mother tongue, Selkirk always declared was the happiest and most wonderful experience of his whole life.

Two and a half years later, after buccaneering in the Pacific and China Sea, the *Duke* with Selkirk aboard, on her way homeward, sailed down the east coast of Scotland, almost within sight of the exile's home. A few days later, on the 14th of October, 1711, the weather-worn ship came up the Thames with the early morning tide, and anchored just below London Bridge.

Very soon, the amazing story of Alexander Selkirk spread across London, then throughout England. The marooned exile became suddenly famous. His story captured the hearts of people everywhere. This popularity frightened Selkirk. So did the London crowds, the noise, the turmoil, and the traffic. He was interviewed by Sir Richard Steele, the writer, and many other notabilities. He told Sir Richard that he didn't like crowds, and wished he were back on his island.

Selkirk found a ship sailing for Leith and he secured a passage aboard. There he found the old folks in the cobbler's shop at Largo. He remained there for a while. He married a dairymaid named Sophia Bruce, and for a brief space he settled down. But his wife died. Then the fever to be voyaging again gripped the returned exile. Once more, Alexander Selkirk went to sea. This time he never returned, but it is believed he died at sea in the year 1721.

The story of *Robinson Crusoe* was given to the world in 1719. How it came to be written is still unknown. But it is believed that Daniel Defoe, who was living in London at this time, had heard the story from Selkirk's own lips.

ROWLAND WALKER.

By courtesy of] [*The Bristol Aeroplane Co., Ltd.*

HIGH ABOVE THE EARTH.

What the earth looks like to the parachutist about to jump.

THE PRINCE OF PARACHUTISTS

OF few airmen may it be said without reflection upon their ability, that they more often landed without their aeroplanes than with them. Yet this was literally true of John Tranum, one of the most daring and expert parachutists that aviation has yet produced.

Tranum was destined to forfeit his life in the most desperate gamble with death ever risked by a parachutist—no less than a drop from a height of five and a half miles above the earth—but before he died, his contempt of danger and wonderful skill had already gained for him the proud title of Prince of Parachutists.

To most airmen the sensation of plunging headlong over the side of an aeroplane with only a silken parachûte between them and death on the earth thousands of feet below, is an experience that they hope never to undergo or, at worst, to suffer only once in a lifetime. To John Tranum, it was the most usual method of leaving an aeroplane. In fact, quite often, he used his parachute to " drop in " on friends, and when invited to spend a week-end at a country house that had no landing-ground, he would engage a pilot to fly him there and then, suitcase in hand, would step over the side to land neatly on a lawn or paddock, to the amazement of his hosts.

John Tranum began his adventurous career as a parachutist in the hardest of all schools, an air circus in America, where spectators were not content with a normal parachute drop—highly dangerous though it was in those early days of unreliable 'chutes—but demanded extra thrills in the form of " stunts " on the way down. The very first stunt that Tranum tried was nearly his last.

Before going up, he tied a cord to the centre of his parachute, his idea being that when the 'chute had opened he could pull it half inside-out, so that it would appear to be crumpling up as he fell faster and faster earthwards. He would then let go of the restraining cord, the 'chute would open out again and the spectators could let go of their chairs.

That was the idea but, in practice, the cord quickly became entangled in the shroud lines of the half opened canopy, and Tranum hurtled earthwards with increasing speed. Frantically, he fought to free the cord, clambering up the shroud-lines to unravel it—and got it loose in the very nick of time. Out flicked the 'chute, the ground rushed up to meet him and he landed with nothing worse than a severe shaking.

He did not try that stunt again, but soon afterwards he had devised another and even more spectacular one, a parachute descent at night illuminated by two great magnesium flares which he would hold in his hands. He made his jump from a height of 3,500 feet, allowed himself to fall clear of the aeroplane before opening his 'chute, and then lit the flares. At once he was engulfed in a searing blaze of white-hot flame that scorched his hands and face and completely blinded him with the intensity of its light. Tranum dropped the flares and landed heavily, blinded and with his clothing on fire, just as the flames were reaching up towards the silken parachute. It was several weeks before his eyes recovered and the first thing he did was to try the same stunt again—but this time he soaked his clothes in fire extinguisher chemical, wore goggles and asbestos gloves and carried the flares attached to broom-handles.

At one time in his career Tranum held the world's records for both the lowest and the highest parachute descents ever made. The lowest jump record was made off a railway-bridge which passed one hundred and fifty-four feet above a dried-up river-bed. A diving board was set up projecting over one side of the bridge and the 'chute was laid out at the far end of the board. A piece of string secured the 'chute to the board and was so arranged that it would automatically open the 'chute and then, its purpose served, break with Tranum's weight as he leapt off the edge of the board. The jump succeeded, but the margin between success and being dashed to death on the rocks of the river-bed was so narrow that Tranum ever afterwards regarded it as the most dangerous jump he had ever made. But at least he had proved that a parachute could safely be used much nearer the ground than was then believed possible, and many pilots, trapped low down in uncontrollable or blazing machines, subsequently owed their lives to his courageous experiment.

His record for the longest drop was made from a height of 20,000 feet above a Californian airport, and in the course of his long descent he encountered a variety of winds at different heights, which first blew him over the coast and out to sea, then back over the airport and towards the Canadian border, and, finally, back to a farmyard near the aerodrome, where he broke his ankle in landing over a six-foot wire fence. He had fallen 19,994 feet in safety only to meet disaster in the last six feet !

But it was as the pioneer of the delayed parachute drop that

[*Graphic Photo Union.*

JOHN TRANUM, WATCH IN HAND, ABOUT TO MAKE A "DELAYED DROP."

Tranum gained, perhaps, his greatest fame and contributed most to the development of parachute design. In a "delayed" drop the airman allows himself to fall unchecked for several thousands of feet before he pulls the ring and releases his parachute, and when Tranum announced his intention of jumping from a height of 20,000 feet and allowing himself to fall unchecked until only 3,000 feet from the ground, there were not lacking experts to tell him he was attempting the impossible. The human heart, they said, would never stand the rapid change of pressure caused by falling from about a quarter sea-level pressure to full sea-level pressure in about ninety seconds. He was warned that he would surely lose consciousness and be unable to release his 'chute. Besides, it was said, no parachute of silk could ever withstand the strain of sudden opening at the speed at which he would be travelling after having fallen nearly 17,000 feet.

But Tranum would not be deterred. He knew, from previous experiments, that a man of average weight falling unchecked through the air attains a maximum speed of about 120 miles an hour, after which his weight is balanced by air pressure and he cannot fall any faster however long he may drop. He knew, too, that he could retain full consciousness during his fall if he wore oxygen-breathing apparatus for use in the rarefied air at high levels. The greatest risk would be whether the silken parachute would stand the sudden opening strain and Tranum, knowing that definite information on this debatable point would be of great value to pilots of high-speed aircraft suddenly forced to abandon their machines, was willing to chance it.

A Hawker Hart day-bomber took him up to the great height of 21,000 feet above Salisbury Plain and then, switching over from the 'plane's oxygen supply to the smaller supply he carried on his back, Tranum stepped from the warmed cockpit out on to the wing—and into a 150 m.p.h. blast of 30 degrees below zero. A nod to the pilot, a final survey of the map-like earth miles below him and he dived head first into space.

Strapped to the palm of one hand he carried a large stop-watch, and as he hurtled earthwards he held this close against his goggled eyes—for only by watching the speeding seconds-hand could he gauge the distance he had fallen and know the moment when he must release his 'chute. For the first mile of his drop he hurtled earthwards in a series of giant somersaults. Then the somersaults grew less frequent, until soon he found himself in the attitude of a diver at

[Fox Photos.

A thrilling moment : will the parachute open ?

an angle of about 45 degrees. His eyes gave him the most trouble, for, despite his goggles, they streamed with water, making it impossible at times for him to see the stop-watch on which his life depended.

At last the seconds-hand showed that he had fallen 17,000 feet, and after allowing himself to drop another two hundred feet for good measure, Tranum jerked the release ring. There was a report like

a gunshot as the parachute cracked open and Tranum felt a searing pain where the harness bit into his flesh as, his fall suddenly checked, he was decelerated from a speed of some two miles a minute to a normal rate of descent. But the 'chute had stood the strain successfully, and Tranum landed a few seconds later, having set a new world's record for a delayed parachute descent.

It was some years before that record was broken, but when it was improved upon, Tranum, now a veteran with several hundreds of delayed drops to his credit, could not resist the challenge to recapture it. This time he planned to drop 25,000 feet before opening his parachute—but it was not his destiny to take that last great gamble with danger.

He set out to make the attempt from Copenhagen aerodrome, but when the aeroplane was five and a half miles above the earth, his main supply of oxygen failed and before he could connect his reserve supply or communicate with his pilot, he became unconscious and was dead when the machine landed.

So passed the Prince of Parachutists, for whom nothing was too daring to attempt and who gave his life in furthering the record of man's achievement—a true pioneer of the air.

T. STANHOPE SPRIGG.

DESCENT BY PARACHUTE.
After a few descents the parachutist treats his "drop" as quite an everyday affair.

[Fox Photos.

"From every available angle the fire had to be fought."

"FIRE! FIRE!"

An Episode During a London Fire.

AT three minutes before seven in the evening of a winter's night, two fire alarms attached to Redcross Street fire-station were pulled by policemen who had noticed a fire.

Instantly helmets and belts were donned, the firemen leapt on to the engines, the great doors flew open, and the engines sped away, the clanging of the bells warning constables, motorists, van-drivers and pedestrians all along the route.

In a very few minutes the first engine arrived. Others from surrounding fire-stations were at their heels. The narrow, crowded streets of Moorfields, lying east and west of Moorgate and Finsbury Pavement, London, with their tall warehouses, shops, factories and tenements, make it a difficult area for fire-fighting even in the day time. This was a dark February night.

The fire was easily located, however. A big four-story building was ablaze. The workrooms, offices, stores and showrooms of a city firm of fancy silk bag manufacturers were already burning fiercely when the first engine arrived. Dense smoke hung like a pall about the factory, the deep interior well, or area, and the narrow street. And the police rushed to the place had no little trouble in clearing a way for the engines.

It was a big blaze. Lurid jets of flame shot out from the smoke. The contents of the store-rooms burned fiercely. Tongues of fire came through the upper windows, then from the roof. From every available angle the fire had to be fought. Streams of water were poured in. The escapes were run up, and water-towers brought into play. Sub-officer Lapham and several other firemen worked from the fourth story and the roof.

It was then the human drama began. The roof suddenly collapsed, and Sub-officer Lapham fell with it ten feet on to the topmost floor. This floor was now alight, and the room was also filled with dense smoke. Scrambling out of the burning débris that had fallen with him, the sub-officer, half-suffocated, dashed through the blinding smoke towards a window.

He had seen from the roof that a balcony ran along this floor outside the window, and made a desperate effort to cut his way through the window and reach it. Blinded by the smoke, he made a slight error of judgment. The balcony began further along. But, driven by the fierce flames behind him, he dropped from the window . . . into the deep central lighting area of the building. Down, down he went more than fifty feet, crashing head first through a corrugated iron roof at ground level into the débris of the basement. And there he lay for some minutes, stunned, half-suffocated and helpless.

The officers and men on the roof who first missed him and heard the crash, then realised what had happened.

"The sub-officer!" they shouted. "He's fallen right down into the area!"

Despite the flames, the smoke, and the imminent peril in which every man up aloft shared, immediate efforts were made to rescue Lapham, though it seemed as if he must have fallen to his death. The difficulties were intense. Owing to smoke and flames, it was impossible to see where Lapham lay sixty feet below. Ladders were lowered, but reached only part of the way down.

An officer decided to try some other way, and the only way was through the burning building. Fireman Kelly saw that the officer had only one man with him and volunteered his help. An attempt was made to get through the basement, but it was full of water and floating stock, and eventually the three struggled across the ground-floor and by pulling away the stock and fixtures, found a window looking into the lighting area.

It was then that Kelly, who had won the Military Medal during the Great War, made a great resolve:

"Lower me into the basement, Sir," he begged of his officer. "I'll try to find him."

Immediately a line was made fast under Kelly's arms. He was then lowered into the lighting area. Reaching the burning roof, he located the hole through which the sub-officer had fallen. Dropping through, he reached the basement, and by the light of the flames around him found Lapham lying in the water. Quickly, he fastened his own line about the injured man and shouted back through the hole in the roof:

[Photopress.

"It was a big blaze."

"I've found him, Sir! Drop me another line, quickly."

A second line was dropped. Kelly then made both lines fast about the body of the helpless officer.

"Hoist away!" he shouted.

The injured sub-officer was then hoisted to safety.

The big blaze was at its worst now. At any moment it was expected that the walls might crash in. But, down in that well area, Fireman Kelly had to wait until another rope could be sent down, and dropped through the hole in the area roof to reach him. Every other exit was barred. There was no way of escape for the imprisoned fireman save by another hoist-rope.

Hissing, burning débris fell through the hole in the roof about him. Moreover, tons of water from the engines poured down through the building into the enclosed area. The water rose to three feet, then it reached his arm-pits, still rising rapidly. Calmly he waited, half-suffocated by smoke, and unable to see whether help was coming even. Those moments must have seemed hours to the imprisoned hero.

His was the courage of grit and endurance. All that time he was looking into the face of death. Would it be death by fire and suffocation, by drowning in the rising waters, or would he be buried alive under the collapsing walls? Then, when human endurance had almost reached its limits, there came a welcome hail through the dense pall of smoke and the tongues of flame overhead:

"Are you there, Kelly?"

"Here!" gasped the half-choked fireman.

"We're lowering a rope! Catch hold!"

The firemen working above had never for a moment forgotten their comrade. That would have been impossible for the London Fire Brigade. But it had taken time and persistence to get another line into position and to lower it through that smoke screen through the hole in the burning roof.

At length, however, the life-line reached the imprisoned man. Fireman Kelly was hoisted out of the well, hauled to safety, then rushed to hospital in a state of utter collapse.

Within another ten days he was back at his post.

"*Mere routine!*" the London Fire Brigade would describe it. "*It's all in the day's work!*"

ROWLAND WALKER.

[Fox Photos.

" THE ROOF SUDDENLY COLLAPSED."

Keystone.

SEA SCOUTS AT WORK.

"LOOK AFTER ARNOLD"

PATROL LEADER D. S. WATSON, of the 33rd Fulham (Sea Scout) Group, was proud of the " Kayak " he had built himself. The kayak was a light, two-seated craft, made after the style of the canoes of that name used by the Eskimoes, and was voted a top-hole specimen by the officers and scouts of the whole Group. The seventeen-years-old Patrol Leader had made a good job of it and on Sunday, March 15th, 1936, he had the kayak at the Troop Headquarters.

" Going out in her, Watson ? " asked Scout Allen Arnold.

" Yes, just for a short spin," was the reply.

" Let me come with you, will you ? "

Patrol Leader Watson looked steadily at the eager thirteen-years-old Scout and smiled. He was fond of the lad and pleased at being asked if he would take the boy as passenger.

" All right, Arnold," he agreed. " But we shall have to ask Mr. Nicholson first."

The Group Scoutmaster readily gave permission : he knew the older boy's capabilities and that he was to be trusted.

" Go ahead, Watson," he exclaimed. " Take care, of course, and mind you don't get cold—it's not Summer yet, you know. Don't go too far and mind you look after Arnold."

The two Scouts went off and carefully boarded the kayak. Care was very necessary, for kayaks have very little beam and any sudden or awkward movement may easily mean a " ducking." Soon they were safely out on the Thames, slipping swiftly down the river as Watson plied the two-bladed paddle.

" Where are we going ? " asked Arnold.

" Down to *The Hawk,*" answered Watson.

Arnold was satisfied with the reply. He knew that *The Hawk* was a barge that was moored off the Chelsea Embankment. It was quite a good run and, with the return trip, quite long enough for a March day. They were thoroughly enjoying themselves.

The barge was reached and soon they were on their way back to their Headquarters. The kayak was behaving well and Watson was more than pleased with it when, without warning, the craft rolled over and the lads found themselves in the water. Luckily they were thrown clear, but the water was cold and they were both fully dressed.

Each of them could swim—they would not have been allowed to

go afloat otherwise—and Watson kept close by his young brother Scout as they struck out for the shore. After a while, seeing that Arnold was tiring, the Patrol Leader told the lad to hold on to him.

Ashore, Scout Frederick Cook saw the swimmers, who appeared to be making good progress, and swam out himself. He relieved Watson, who was still going well, of his charge and rapidly carried Arnold to the shore, out-distancing the Patrol Leader.

Suddenly, when quite close to the shore, Watson disappeared, apparently worn out by the cold and his efforts to keep his promise to "look after Arnold." Group Scoutmaster Nicholson and Assistant Scoutmaster Monk, who happened to be near, both dived into the river in an endeavour to find Watson, but without success. The Patrol Leader had given his life to save the younger Scout.

Patrol Leader Watson was posthumously awarded the Bronze Cross, the highest Scout award for Gallantry.

JOHN F. C. WESTERMAN.

"Without warning the craft rolled over."

ZEEBRUGGE

DURING the dark days of March and April 1918, when the German Army on the Western Front was sweeping the Allies back towards the old 1914 battlefields, it was left to the British Navy to redeem the position, at least for a time, by an attack on the enemy's naval bases at Zeebrugge and Ostend.

Admiral Sir Roger Keyes and his staff planned the attack. Its strongest point was its sheer audacity : a close second was the carefully thought out preparation by the Admiral.

Zeebrugge and Ostend were the ports from which the German torpedo boats and U boats could raid the shipping in the English Channel. The coup was planned to bottle up the bases and render them inoperative.

On April 22nd, 1918, *H.M.S. Vindictive,* two Liverpool ferry boats, the *Iris* and the *Daffodil,* together with three obsolete cruisers, the *Intrepid, Iphigenia* and *Thetis,* and a mosquito fleet of destroyers, motor launches, coastal motorboats and one submarine, C-3, steamed slowly out and headed towards Zeebrugge with its canal and great half-moon-shaped Mole.

That night, some fifteen miles from their objective, they took up their formation for the attack. The night was dark and offered nearly ideal conditions—a drift of haze helping considerably to screen their approach.

H.M.S. Vindictive had been towing the *Iris* and the *Daffodil.* She cast them off to steam on their own and the three ships went ahead to carry out the first phase of the attack, the *Intrepid,* the *Iphigenia* and the *Thetis* following some distance astern. Their turn was to come later.

All went well until the *Vindictive* was close to the Mole. Then the wind lulled and veered, sweeping back the smokescreen the ships were using, to reveal the warship with her landing parties of bluejackets and marines standing ready for the attack. At once the darkened harbour became a blaze of light. Star shells soared up, the beams of the searchlights swung and played on the advancing vessels and the incessant flashes of gunfire made the night as light as day.

Guns and machine-guns along the Mole and on the shore batteries woke to life and it was through a veritable gale of shelling that the

" Star shells soared up, the beams of se

Vindictive put her bows against the thirty-feet high concrete Mole, let go an anchor and signalled to the *Daffodil* to push her stern in. The *Iris* endeavoured to help her sister ship.

Along the port side of the *Vindictive* was a high false deck, designed to give the eighteen gangways she carried sufficient height easily to bridge the gap between the ship and the top of the Mole. The men were mustered on the main and lower decks. The gangways were lowered and they scraped and rebounded on the parapet as the *Vindictive* rolled. Before the order to land had been given, Colonel Elliot and Captain Halahan were killed by shell and machine-gun fire. They were to have led the assaulting force. Other officers took their places.

The landing on the Mole was a perilous business. The men had to cross the splintering gangways, drop over the parapet into the

ung and played on the advancing vessels."

fire of German machine-guns which swept its length and jump down a further sixteen feet to the surface of the Mole itself. The coloured picture facing page 192 represents an artist's impression of the landing, painted from a vivid description by one of the surviving officers of the *Vindictive*. It gives some slight idea of the difficulties which had to be overcome by the gallant officers and men of the landing party. Men were killed and wounded in dozens as they crowded along the gangways, but nothing could stop the orderly landing.

The *Vindictive's* lower deck was a shambles as the Commander made his rounds, but wounded and dying men raised themselves to cheer as he passed by. Three full crews had been killed on the howitzer mounted forward, but there was always a new crew to man it. Aft, in the stern cabin, a firework expert, who had never been to sea before, was firing big rockets out of a port-hole to illuminate the darkened lighthouse at the end of the Mole to guide the other ships in.

After helping to berth the *Vindictive,* the *Daffodil* was to have landed her men, but Captain Carpenter, the Commander of the *Vindictive,* ordered her to remain where she was, keeping the cruiser pressed against the stonework.

Meanwhile the *Iris* was having trouble. Her grapnels were not large enough to span the parapet. Two of her officers, Lieutenant-Commander Bradford and Lieutenant Hawkins climbed ashore in the face of an inferno of shot and shell and tried to make the grapnels fast, but both were killed.

At last the *Iris* was compelled to drop astern of the *Vindictive,* where, sheltered by the cruiser, she managed to berth alongside. She suffered heavily in the process, losing eight officers and sixty-nine men killed and three officers and one hundred and two men wounded.

The landing parties met with no resistance from the enemy, apart from the intense and unceasing fire. They knew exactly what they had to do, where each building or other objective was situated and went to their appointed task in perfect order. One by one the

"A motor launch immediately dashed in and took off the remainder of her crew."

"All went well until the *Vindictive* was close to the Mole."

marked buildings were demolished by dynamite in spite of the hail of bullets.

As they worked and attracted the German forces, the *Thetis* steamed into the harbour. Only a remnant of her crew were left in her: the others had been taken off by motor launches outside the harbour, but the remainder kept her guns going. She cleared a string of armed barges that defended the channel, but unluckily fouled a net defence with one of her propellers. Unable to steer properly in consequence and pounded by shellfire, she found herself in a sinking condition some hundreds of yards from the canal, which was her objective. Her Commander, after signalling directions to the following ships, exploded the prepared charges in her bottom and sank her. A motor launch immediately dashed in and took off the remainder of her crew.

Next came the *Intrepid*. She carried a full crew: the motor launches had failed to get alongside before she entered the harbour, so she had men enough for anything and showed it by the intensity of her gunfire. Her Commander put the bows of his ship on the mud of the western bank of the canal entrance, swung her stern round until it was across the water-way and sunk the gallant old ship in her appointed place. Her crew was safely taken off by fast launches and rushed to safety.

The *Iphigenia* followed close astern—almost too close as it turned out, for smoke from *Intrepid* swept over her, blinding her helmsmen and navigators and making her steer badly. As a result she rammed a dredger and a barge, carrying on with the wreck of the barge across her bows. Soon after a shell cut through the *Intrepid's* steam whistle pipe and the resultant rush of steam cleared the smoke and the *Iphigenia* was able to see again. She was beached on the eastern side of the canal mouth with her stern to the west and sunk with her engines still running to hold her in position. More motor launches slipped alongside and took off her crew.

By this time the shell and bullet-torn harbour was alive with small craft. As they raced back towards the open sea, the rescuers and rescued saw yet another phase of the attack. Lieutenant R. D. Sandford, with a crew of one other officer, Lieutenant Howell-Price, and seven men, approached in the old submarine C-3. His objective was the wooden jetty that connected the shore to the Mole proper. The submarine was crammed full with explosive and her Commander had orders to get as close to the wooden viaduct as possible, fire the fuse, head C-3 for her target and leave her to complete the work by herself, while he and his crew escaped by means of a small motorboat that was being towed astern. The submarine's steering gear had been arranged so that she would steer herself for the last few hundred yards before she blew up.

Lieutenant Sandford and his crew had other ideas, however. They decided that the mission was too delicate to be entrusted to automatic steering, so they took C-3 right up to the viaduct and jammed her nose tightly into the big piles. Strangely enough, hardly a shot greeted them from the masses of German troops on the viaduct as they steamed up. Perhaps their very audacity had stunned the enemy for the time being.

Once in place, the fuse was lit and the crew tumbled into the motorboat. Then their luck changed. It was as if a spell had been broken. Rifle and machine-gun fire lashed all around them and just at that moment the motorboat's propeller fouled some obstruction and was lost. Inside C-3 the lighted fuse was spluttering its way nearer to tons of explosive. Two men seized a pair of oars the boat carried and began pulling as hard as they could. Both fell wounded : others took their places, to fall in their turn. Somehow they managed to cover about two hundred yards before C-3 blew up, shattering the viaduct and sending hundreds of German troops to their death.

Every man in the boat except Lieutenant Howell-Price was

[*Topical.*

" The submarine was crammed full with explosives."

wounded. He continued to pull on the small oars until a steam pinnace dashed up and took the submarine's crew on board. In spite of the tenseness of their own plight, each man on the *Vindictive* and on the Mole stopped fighting and cheered when they heard the explosion that indicated the success of C-3's mission—a tribute from the brave to the brave.

Meanwhile the battle on the Mole continued. The enemy fire had slackened considerably under the punishment that had been meted out to them, but it was still fierce. The demolition parties had

THE CHANNEL INTO ZEEBRUGGE HARBOUR EFFECTIVELY BLOCKED BY THE *THETIS*, THE *INTREPID* AND THE *IPHIGENIA*.

carried out their work and the men began to retire to the *Vindictive* and the *Daffodil.*

In spite of the hail of bullets and shells, practically every man assisted a wounded messmate back to safety, until at length the Mole was successfully evacuated.

There was still a lot to do. Lashed by shellfire, rifle and machine-gun bullets, the ships' crews hauled in the gangways, cast off the grappling irons, unshackled the anchor dropped by the *Vindictive* and, assisted by the redoubtable *Iris* and *Daffodil,* the battered cruiser turned and headed out to sea, her guns flashing and roaring defiance at the enemy.

With her funnels gaping with holes and leaning far out of true, her decks and fittings torn and shattered, the *Vindictive* steamed for home, with streams of flame spouting from her sieve-like smokestacks and showers of sparks sweeping over her decks as her " black-squad " below fed the furnaces and worked her up to a full seventeen knots —a fine accomplishment in view of her battered and shattered condition. Her glorious achievement will live for ever in the annals of the British Navy.

In her wake steamed the equally battered *Iris* and *Daffodil.* Certainly the smaller vessels had been more protected by the high walls of the Mole than their bigger sister, but, from the time they had first been sighted, the ships had been subjected to an unceasing hail of shot and shell from hundreds of guns, yet they were able to steam safely away.

Outside the harbour the ships were greeted by *H. M. S. Warwick* with Admiral Sir Roger Keyes on board. The Admiral had been standing by in the destroyer throughout the action to command operations.

When the ships and " mosquito " craft left Zeebrugge, they had the satisfaction of knowing they had achieved their object and carried out the operation more than well in the face of tremendous odds. They had breached the Mole, blocked the Bruges Canal, destroyed most of the fortifications and many guns and effectively sealed up the harbour, rendering it useless as a base for future operations of hostile ships.

Our illustration, which appears on page 190, is from an actual photograph which appeared at the time in the *Illustrated London News.* It shows a birdseye view of the channel into Zeebrugge harbour, effectively blocked by the sunken *Thetis, Intrepid* and *Iphigenia*.

But they had had to pay a heavy price in casualties, although these casualties were light in view of the circumstances. Every moment of the raid was crowded with acts of heroism and courage, many unseen in the heat of the battle. Later in the year many of those who took part received Victoria Crosses and other decorations, but the general feeling was that those heroes were but representatives of the larger body of heroes who had all more than won the distinctions by their courage and devotion to duty.

As for the ships that took part, the *Vindictive* returned to Ostend later and completed the good work by blocking that harbour with her cement-filled hull, while, as a mark of distinction, the Liverpool ferry boats, *Iris* and *Daffodil,* were honoured by being called the *Royal Iris* and the *Royal Daffodil.*

JOHN F. C. WESTERMAN.

[L.N.A.

The battered *Vindictive* after her glorious exploit.

H.M.S. VINDICTIVE AT ZEEBRUGGE.
The landing on the Mole was a perilous business.

ENGLAND TO NEW ZEALAND IN ELEVEN DAYS

The Stirring Story of the Longest Lone Flight Ever Made by a Woman.

IN the early hours of the morning of October the 4th, 1936, a little group of people stood on the aerodrome at Lympne, in Kent, straining their eyes for a last glimpse at the tail-light of an aeroplane fast disappearing into the night sky above the English Channel.

The aeroplane they watched was a Percival Vega Gull monoplane and alone in its glass-enclosed cabin sat a twenty-seven-year-old New Zealand girl, Jean Batten, bound for the other end of the World in an attempt to do what no man or woman had ever done before—to fly alone from England to New Zealand.

It was a daring adventure, but the girl who was thus bravely attempting it had something more than high courage to assist her. She had also the experience gained in nearly six years of flying, years in which, by a series of remarkable long-distance flights, she had proved herself a pilot of unusual ability. Among the several fine feats already to her credit were a solo flight from England to Australia and back and a lone crossing of the South Atlantic from Africa to South America—all made in a light aeroplane and with that absence of fuss or extravagant publicity which has marked every achievement of this modest young airwoman.

Now she was off on the most ambitious venture of her flying career, a 14,000 miles' flight from England to her home in New Zealand, a journey in which the final lap must be a 1,200 miles' crossing of the featureless wastes of the dreaded Tasman Sea.

Four hours after leaving Lympne, Jean Batten had reached the Mediterranean coast of France and was having a hurried breakfast on the aerodrome at Marseilles. Half an hour later, her machine refuelled, she was in the air again and speeding on towards Italy at a steady 150 miles an hour. Late that afternoon she landed at Brindisi and, having already covered 1,205 miles that day, decided that she had earned a night's rest.

She was up and away at dawn, heading out across the Mediterranean with Baghdad, some 1,500 miles distant, as her objective for the night. Six hours later she landed on the Island of Cyprus, spent a bare half hour in refuelling and was off again, bound for the Syrian coast and Asia. All through that afternoon she sped above the sandy wastes of Syria and Irak, fighting a powerful headwind which so delayed her progress that she was finally forced to land in the gathering darkness some 200 miles short of Baghdad. The desert station of a petroleum company gave her hospitality for the night and next day, making her usual dawn start, she flew 440 miles to Basra, at the head of the Persian Gulf, for breakfast. It was a quick breakfast, snatched in intervals of checking over her engine, for Jean Batten was determined to dine in India that night and a wide stretch of Persia lay between her and her goal.

She achieved her purpose and at 7 o'clock that evening brought her Gull down to a perfect landing on Karachi aerodrome after a nine hours' non-stop flight during which she had covered 1,240 miles and run the gauntlet of raging dust storms in the region of Jask, which at times had forced her up to over 12,000 feet to avoid their blinding embrace. Her total mileage for the day was 1,682, the best she had yet achieved and she had reached India within three days of leaving England.

But the following day was to eclipse even this fine achievement for, leaving Karachi just before 4 o'clock in the morning, Jean flew right across the vast continent of India to land that night at Akyab, in Burma, on the eastern coast of the Bay of Bengal. She made only one stop *en route*, at Allahabad, and set a new record for her daily mileage with a total of 1,700 miles flown in the day.

From Akyab she flew next day to Penang and on this 1,150 miles flight she encountered the worst weather of the entire journey. Trapped by torrential rainstorms near Alor Star, she was forced to fly " blind " for hours on end, guided solely by the instruments in her cockpit and with all sight of land or sea blotted out by the driving sheets of water. So great was the violence of the storm that the fabric of one of the wings was ripped open in several places and Jean Batten had some anxious moments wondering whether the damage would spread and weaken the entire wing structure. But she carried on and, resisting the temptation to land at Rangoon, flew on to land in the afternoon at Penang, having covered 1,150 miles non-stop. A few minutes later she was off again and flew 300 miles to Singapore, where she landed for a brief rest while ready helpers carried out repairs to the damaged wing.

[Keystone (L.E.A.).

Jean Batten adjusting the propeller of her machine.

When darkness fell, mechanics prepared to house the machine for the night but, to their surprise, Jean Batten, tired but undaunted by the dawn-to-dusk flight she had just completed, announced her intention of resuming the journey that night. She rested for a few hours at the aerodrome and just before midnight took-off from the flood-lit aerodrome at Singapore and headed south for the Dutch East Indies on the first night flight of her record-breaking journey.

The early dawn of October the 10th, the fifth full day since she had left England, saw her passing low over Batavia. She did not land, but kept on to Rambang, in Java, where she came down for a hurried meal at 9 o'clock in the morning. Almost immediately she left for Koepang, where a punctured tail wheel threatened to cause a serious delay in her triumphal progress. But Jean Batten was not easily defeated and with the damaged tyre stuffed with sponges she was off with the dawn next day on the last and most dangerous lap of the journey to Australia—the long crossing of the shark-infested waters of the Timor Sea.

By courtesy of] [*The Percival Aircraft, Ltd.*

"Flying for hour after hour, far out of sight of land."

Flying for hour after hour, far out of sight of land and guided only by her compass, Jean Batten kept a true course for the Australian coast and just before 11 o'clock that morning, was circling Port Darwin, on the mainland, preparing to land. Then she came near disaster. As the Gull glided in to land, the throttle lever suddenly jammed open, and with the engine running full out, Jean Batten was forced to climb up again and circle round the aerodrome while she struggled with the lever. On the second attempt, skilful piloting and violent use of the wheel-brakes succeeded in getting and keeping the machine safely on the ground. The engine was quickly switched off and a triumphant Jean Batten, looking as spick and span as the day she left Lympne, emerged from the cabin. She had flown from England to Australia in a total elapsed time of 5 days, 21 hours, 3 minutes, and had beaten the previous record for a solo flight over the same route by the handsome margin of nearly 24 hours.

Four days later, having flown right across the Australian continent from north to south, Jean Batten was waiting at Richmond aerodrome, near Sydney, for favourable weather in which to set off over the Tasman Sea on the last lap of her journey to New Zealand. So perilous is this long oversea crossing that many people had tried to persuade her to abandon the attempt.

But Jean Batten, though she promised to wait for good weather, was not to be dissuaded from the task she had set herself, and in the early morning of October the 16th the Gull passed out over the Australian coast, heading out into the blue on its 1,200 miles over-water flight to New Zealand.

A cable from Sydney to Auckland announced her departure and then for hours that seemed like days to the people of Auckland waiting to welcome their countrywoman, there was silence. Eight and a half hours passed—the time that Jean herself had estimated it would take her to make the crossing—and still there was no news of the lone flier. A silence fell upon the great multitude that had gathered on Auckland aerodrome and into the minds of all came the thought of that vast empty ocean, the Tasman Sea.

Nine and a half hours had gone by when at last there came news that the Gull, delayed by head winds, had been sighted off New Plymouth, the exact point at which Jean Batten had been aiming over a thousand miles of ocean. An hour later the Gull had landed at Auckland and Jean Batten, heroine of the longest lone flight ever made by a woman, maker of the first solo flight from England to New Zealand, and holder of the England-Australia speed record, was home at last!

T. STANHOPE SPRIGG.

[*Wide World Photos.*

Jean Batten making final adjustments to her plane.

THE DEATHLESS STORY OF RORKE'S DRIFT

THERE is one half-forgotten epic of British heroism, endurance and self-sacrifice which our modern history books seldom mention. It is the deathless story of *Rorke's Drift,* where, one day, a handful of British soldiers under the command of a mere youth, Lieutenant John Chard, of the Royal Engineers, saved a whole British colony from massacre.

It happened on the 22nd of January, in the year 1879. Rorke's Drift is a river ford on the Buffalo, just below the junction of Blood River, which, a little lower down, becomes the Tugela. The Zulus, fiercest and most warlike of all the native tribes in South Africa, after ruthlessly attacking the surrounding tribes, killing men, women and children, began to threaten the British settlements in Natal. The danger became so real that the British colonists began to arm themselves in defence of their homes, then sent urgent appeals for help to Cape Colony, and also to England.

The storm broke suddenly. A colonist in shirt sleeves, his mount bathed in foam and sweat, rode in with this message : *Cetywayo, with* 30,000 *Zulu warriors, is advancing upon Natal.*

The Zulus, armed with muskets, spears, and assegais, athirst for more blood after subduing their neighbouring tribes, had resolved to push their conquests further south, and to wipe out utterly the white settlements. Every available British soldier and fighting colonist was rushed northward to the border, and a mixed force of 700 soldiers and 131 colonists crossed the Buffalo River at Rorke's Drift to hold up the Zulu advance.

The column marched toward Isandhlwana (Isandula), some ten miles beyond the river. But all the sick men, some twenty-three in number were left at the Drift, where there was a little wooden hospital, a commissariat store, and a temporary pontoon across the stream, under the command of Lieutenant John Chard.

Defend the Drift to the last man ! was the special order given to Chard.

Rorke's Drift was, therefore, a most important post. Supplies were to be sent forward from there. Sick men and wounded were to be sent back there, while the ponts and flying bridge formed the only safe crossing now the Buffalo River was in flood. So a Company of

"EXCEPT FOR ABOUT HALF-A-DOZEN MEN WHO WERE ON OUTPOST AND MANAGED TO RIDE THROUGH THE ZULU CHARGES, NOT A MAN WAS LEFT ALIVE."

THE RELIEF COLU

1. The Reverend Mr. Witts's house with redoubt of mealie-bags and biscuit tins.   2. The hospital bur

ING AT RORKE'S DRIFT. [From a Contemporary Drawing.

. The cattle kraal. 4. Tyana Mountain. 5. Lieutenant-Colonel Russell leading the relief column.

the 24th Foot, under Lieutenant Bromhead, were also left behind to aid Chard in his defence of the Drift.

Then dawned that momentous day, the 22nd of January, and the African sun shone down upon that little British encampment at Rorke's Drift. There was never a thought of approaching peril. The column which had crossed the Buffalo River was between the enemy and the camp. The sentries down in the gully by the ponts and the flying bridge had been changed, and the day wore on toward afternoon. Then fell the thunderbolt out of the clear African sky.

Horsemen galloping toward the Drift! came a cry.

It seems as if Private Henry Hook, one of the hospital orderlies, who afterwards received the V.C. for that day's work, gave the first warning. Hook, who belonged to the 24th Foot, was cooking tea for the sick men at a stove in the open air, when he espied the little dust cloud on the other side of the river. Instantly, Chard turned his glasses toward the spot. Out of the dust he saw the two horsemen emerge. One of them was hatless and coatless, with a revolver strapped round his breast. A few minutes later, their horses breathing hard and almost exhausted, the men crossed the ponts, and Chard recognised one of them. "It's Adendorff!" he said, "Lieutenant Adendorff! And the other's one of the Natal Carabineers!"

The men reined in, but only for a moment.

"Bad news!" cried Adendorff. "The entire column has been destroyed."

"Destroyed?"

"Massacred!" panted Adendorff. "A most awful disaster. Except about half-a-dozen of us, who were on outpost, and managed to ride through the Zulu charges, not a man has been left alive!"

"Good God! Where did it happen, Lieutenant?"

"At Isandula . . . ten miles away. Twenty thousand Zulus surrounded us, and our men fought like Trojans. But it wasn't any use. They were more than twenty to one, and the devils were mad for blood. They broke through our square, trampled over our men, stabbing and yelling like fiends. Now they're coming here . . . !"

"Coming here?" asked Chard, coolly.

"Yes, like the fiends in hell. I've ridden like the deuce to warn you. Now I'm going on to warn Helpmakaar and the other settlements." And with this hurried message, Lieutenant Adendorff and the Carabineer, who seemed almost demented by their terrible experiences that day, dug their spurs into their jaded horses and left Rorke's Drift behind.

The bad news spread like wildfire through the little British camp, thence to the sick men in the little hospital. But the young officer in command rose to the occasion.

" Order the men to fall in, Bromhead ! " he said.

A moment later, the bugler of the 24th Foot sounded the assembly,

" From across the Drift there came first a dull, distant roar as of a torrent advancing."

and every soldier, cook, hospital orderly, and commissariat-stores man fell in. The rest, some native allies from a near-by kraal, and a few miscellaneous camp followers, including a few *white men*, did not answer that bugle call. The news of the Isandula massacre had scared them. They were unwilling to face the approaching fiends. They had already fled south, leaving Chard and his remnant of heroes to defend the sick and dying men in the hospital, and to hold the Drift.

There wasn't a minute to spare. And Chard's words were few as he turned to address the ranks. " My orders were to defend Rorke's Drift, boys ! " he said. " And besides the river crossing, the hospital is full of sick men. Will you stand by me ? "

" Yes-s."

There was a tremendous cheer from so small a company.

" To the last man ? "

" Yes-s-s ! "

" Then listen ! The devils will be here any minute now. We must loophole the hospital and stores, build a barricade with mealie bags and biscuit tins, make a lager and form square within ! "

Every man got down to his job. Two waggons were drawn across to form a sort of connecting barricade between the hospital and the stores. Some men hurriedly began to loophole the little buildings, others to pile the mealie bags and biscuit tins into a rude square, behind which they were to fight, and if needs be, to die at their posts . . . which many of them did.

The men worked feverishly with Chard directing at every point. The youthful Royal Engineer was a master of his craft. He left nothing to chance. As soon as the outer barricade with the mealie bags, and other odds and ends had taken shape, he said : " Now lads, let's build a smaller barricade inside the square." Although he didn't say so in words, Chard knew full well that, as the fight went on towards the finish, he would probably have to defend the post with a mere handful of survivors.

They had got the second barricade only two biscuit tins high, however, when from across the Drift there came first a dull, distant roar as of a torrent advancing, then the fierce, blood-curdling yell of 3,000 frenzied Zulu warriors, every one of them intent upon a second massacre before the sun set that day.

" Every man to his post ! " was the next order. A few more notes on the bugle recalled the sentries from the ponts. Chard had need of every man who could use a weapon. Then the heroic 24th, under the immediate supervision of their Company officer, Lieutenant Bromhead, formed square within the first barricade, except six men who had been told off to defend the sick men within the hospital. Altogether, Chard had eighty men of the 24th Foot, and including himself, Surgeon Reynolds, Mr. Dalton and the men of the Commissariat, another sixteen. In addition, there were the twenty-three sick men in the hospital, some of whom were very ill.

" Don't waste your fire ! " came Chard's order. " Wait till the enemy charge ! " A few moments later, the Zulu warriors, having crossed the Drift, and having completely surrounded the little garrison, first fired their muskets, then yelling like fiends unleashed from hell, charged down in a solid mass upon the defenders.

" Fire ! "

A wall of flame leapt from the outer barricade. But although the Zulus fell in heaps, fierce, yelling warriors leapt over the bodies of the slain, and charged right up to the muzzles of the British rifles.

[Central Press.

A Zulu *Impi* on the march.

Some of the dark-skinned warriors, who seemed to know no fear, leapt the barricades and were killed within the square. The air was thick with flying assegais, and already the death roll within the barricades began to mount. There was no retreat for that little garrison, however. Every man, in this life-and-death struggle, fought like a hero. And at length that first, fierce wave of Zulus recoiled. They fell back, carrying off hundreds of wounded, but leaving the ground littered with their dead.

A welcome respite followed. But it lasted only minutes. Quarter of an hour later, urged on by their great warrior chief, Dabulamanzi, brother of King Cetywayo, the Zulus charged again. This time the assailants captured the cook-house, several outbuildings, and set the thatched roof of the hospital ablaze. Also, the musketry fire of the Zulus from cover of the outbuildings was so fierce now that Chard withdrew his men behind the second barricade of biscuit tins. At this moment it really seemed as if the fate of the tiny garrison, fighting against odds of thirty to one, was sealed.

The fury of the enemy increased. The wild yells of the warriors almost drowned the rattle of the continuous firing. The final massacre, to the Zulus at least, seemed assured. But, no! A third and a fourth time, the fiercest warriors Africa has ever produced, recoiled from that wall of fire. But it was only for a brief space. On they came again and still again.

The sun went down . . . but the fight still continued by the blazing light of the burning hospital. At midnight the battle was still raging, with the garrison growing steadily weaker but defiant as ever. Meanwhile, under that blazing roof only a few yards away, deeds of amazing heroism that almost stagger the imagination, were being performed by four privates of the 24th Foot.

Let their names be mentioned here, for every one of them gained the V.C. that day. They were:

Private John Williams,
,, Henry Hook,
,, Robert Jones,
,, William Jones.

Bromhead had detailed six men to guard the hospital. Two of them were killed almost at the beginning of the fight. The remaining four carried on.

When the Zulus beat in the hospital door, the two Jones dashed toward the opening, crossed their bayonets, and killed every warrior who tried to cross the threshold. And this desperate fight to save the sick men from death and mutilation went on all the time Williams and Hook were carrying or dragging the sick and wounded men to safety.

All this time the blazing roof was falling in. The place was thick with fire and smoke. Musket balls, spears and assegais spattered the doorway, now piled high with enemy dead and wounded. Robert Jones had three assegai wounds, and the other doorkeeper was also wounded. But neither man left his post. And never a single Zulu entered that doorway until every sick man had been evacuated.

Twenty of the sick men were carried safely within the barricade. Two fever patients disappeared during the mêlée, and the last man, helpless with a broken leg, was dragged through a hole in the wall by Private Williams under heavy fire . . . his leg being broken again in the process. Then, as the last blazing rafters fell in, the two heroic door-keepers, their work done, limped wounded through a hail of bullets to the shelter of the barricade . . . and the cheers of their comrades.

All that night, until dawn broke away to eastward, Chard and Bromhead, with the remnant of the little garrison, fought on at the barricade. Then, about seven in the morning, just as the Zulus were preparing for one grand, final rush, which was to end the battle, a British relief column was seen hurrying to the spot, and the enemy drew off.

That was the end of the famous fight. The post had been held. And there can be no doubt that Chard's heroic defence of Rorke's Drift that day, stemmed the fierce tide of the great Zulu invasion of Natal, and saved the British settlements from massacre. The tragedy of Isandhula had cast a gloom over the whole British nation. But the heroic defence of Rorke's Drift by that gallant little band made every heart in England beat with pride.

Lieutenant Chard, in his modest despatch, praised everybody but himself. But, when Sir Garnet Wolsey arrived in South Africa, some months later, to take over command of the Zulu expedition, he made Lieutenant Chard a Captain and a Brevet-Major of the British Army, and, at a great inspection of the troops, the famous general pinned the V.C. on to Chard's breast.

When the Zulu rising had been suppressed, Cetywayo deposed, and the fierce warrior tribe brought under British protection, later that year, Chard returned to England, where he received a tremendous ovation. The whole nation wished to honour him. Queen Victoria commanded his attendance at Balmoral, while the folk in his native Devonshire presented him with a sword of honour.

And yet, after all, *Rorke's Drift* is just one of those countless, half-forgotten epics of heroism, endurance and self-sacrifice, upon which the British Commonwealth of Nations has been built.

ROWLAND WALKER.

By courtesy of] [*The Bristol Aeroplane Co., Ltd.*

BRISTOL FIGHTERS BOMBING A GERMAN AERODROME IN THE GREAT WAR.

RICHTHOFEN'S LAST FIGHT

THE tragedy of the Great War of 1914-18 is now passing into history. But, out of the smoke-screen of those terrible years, epic stories of personal courage, self-sacrifice and devotion to duty will always cast a gleam upon those dark days when the future hung so heavy with fate.

The story of our British airmen alone, in the pages of history, will be one of undying fame. When that story is fully told, generations yet unborn will stand aghast at their heroism, endurance and grit.

Many of our British airmen were mere boys fresh from school. Scores of them were still in their teens when they fought the most amazing duels in the air. McCubbin was eighteen and a half, when in June, 1916, he fought and crashed the crack German ace, Immelmann. Yet at that time, six months or more before Richthofen's star began to rise, Immelmann was the most daring and successful of all the German air-fighters.

There were others, also mere boys, who were equally resourceful and daring. A dozen books would scarce suffice for half their thrilling deeds. Captain Ball, a youth of twenty, would sally out alone, sail calmly through the barrage of shrapnel and poison fumes and attack the first German formation he met. There may have been ten, fifteen or twenty enemy machines in the formation. It made no difference to this young air-fiend. He was always at his best fighting alone. He had that wonderful synchronisation of eye and brain which, linked with a fearless courage, makes the fighting ace. When he had broken up the enemy formation, crashed three or four German machines, Ball would coolly sail out of the mêlée back over the lines unscathed.

Bishop was yet another young air fighter who fought best alone. Out he would go into the chilly dawn, cross the lines, search out an enemy aerodrome twenty or thirty miles behind the front, and attack it single handed with bomb and machine-gun. There were many others . . . Barker, McCudden and McKeever . . . amongst the young British airmen. Nothing in the spacious days of Drake and Cromwell, of Wolfe or Nelson can surpass their fearless deeds.

Britain was at death grips with a powerful and ruthless foe. All the things our fathers fought for were at stake. For four fearful years the freedom of men and nations, the heritage of the ages, hung in the balance. As the weary months dragged on and the sinking of unarmed merchantmen continued, and the spectre of famine loomed before every English home, even brave men were filled with despair.

"Only one thing can save us from final defeat and disaster!" declared the experts. This was when the armies were landlocked and the merciless submarine was at its worst: "We must gain supremacy in the air."

It was the almost reckless daring and abandon of young airmen of the McCudden, Ball, and Bishop type that, towards the end of the third year of the war, made final victory for the Allies possible.

At first, the German air arm had been overwhelming. Later, especially after the formation of the R.A.F. under Air Marshal Trenchard, the German air squadrons were fought over their own side of the line. The German railheads, bridges, ammunition dumps, and troop concentrations were bombed almost daily.

But the end was not yet. A new star had risen in the German firmament. It was Rittmeister Manfred von Richthofen. He was the most brilliant air-fighter Germany ever produced. He was a superb aerial duellist. The German H.Q. credited him with having brought down eighty British and French airmen.

He rallied the failing esprit de corps of the German Flying Corps. He formed the famous "Richthofen Circus," which consisted of some sixty of the most famous German air-fighters. In his red *Albatross* or *Fokker*, and followed by his "circus," nicknamed by the British the "Tango Party," he would suddenly appear, almost darkening the heavens, and attack any point along the battle line with bomb and machine-gun, then as quickly he would disappear before British air-fighters could reach the scene.

In 1917 the Richthofen Circus had become a serious menace. Richthofen himself had become a man of mystery, almost a legend. British aces went out to hunt for him and couldn't find him. Yet the Red Devil was a clean fighter. And because of that the British airmen honoured him. They even drank his health in the Mess . . . and prayed to meet him.

It was a strange thing, that chivalry of the air during the Great War, when the barbarities on sea and land were probably greater than in any previous war. But *clean fighting* was an almost unbroken rule both in the British and German Flying Corps.

Once, after a terrific air duel with an English pilot, Richthofen at length crashed his man behind the German lines. That same night in the Mess, he was describing the fight to his friend Voss, another ace. "Did you kill the verdammt Englander?" asked Voss.

"No," replied the Red Baron. "But I went down to thirty feet to have a look at him." (Often the victorious airman landed to help his wounded enemy if no assistance seemed near.)

[Topical (L.E.A.).

Baron von Richthofen.

"And what did the Englander do?"

"He dared me to land. Swung up his pivot gun and began blazing away at me. Thought I wanted to take him prisoner. He shot a score of holes in my machine. He was some fighter that Britisher."

"Didn't you finish him off?" asked Voss.

"No! I had crashed him. That was enough."

It reads like a story of the Round Table. Arthur's knights never showed more chivalry than this; it explains why Richthofen, even when he was taking such toll of the Allied airmen, was such a favourite in the Messes of the British Flying Corps. This clean fighting between the aerial duellists on both sides is, perhaps, the one rift of blue in a very dark and tragic page of history.

Then came the day of Richthofen's last fight. Although the Red Baron had now become, for the whole German nation at least, the *Ace of Trumps*, and seemed to be utterly invincible in the air the end came quite suddenly, during one of his famous dog-fights, when the sky was almost black with some forty or fifty machines of his famous "Tango Party."

It was on Sunday, the 21st of April, 1918, about one thousand yards from the village of Bonnay, on the road to Corbie, during the retreat of the Fifth British Army on the St. Quentin front, that the Red Baron met his death.

Hindenburg had just delivered his most smashing blow of the whole war. It was the last big effort of the mailed fist to break through the British lines, capture Amiens and Paris, then seize the Channel ports. And it nearly succeeded. Some forty-four German divisions, some of them fresh from their crashing victories on the Russian and Italian fronts, were hurled upon the fourteen British divisions holding the extended lines of the St. Quentin front.

Shot down, but uninjured, a German airman salutes his conqueror.

As this thunderbolt, which bent back but did not break the British line, fell, a call went out for a supreme effort to Richthofen and the whole German Flying Corps. The Richthofen Circus, although latterly its fighting had been mainly done behind the German lines, made a magnificent response.

On the morning of April the 21st, the Circus crossed the British lines near Corbie, fighting hard with two British R.E.8 machines which had been spotting for the guns. Suddenly, amid the rattle of machine-guns and the roar of at least forty propellers, six British *Camels* of 209 Squadron arrived like bolts from the blue and flung themselves into the fight.

It must have been one of the last and biggest dog-fights of the whole war. Down below, from Villers Bretonneux to Corbie on the Somme, thousands of British Tommies, infantry and artillery, looked on and cheered.

Once the dog-fight really began, the anti-aircraft guns became silent. Friend and

" Captain Brown also dived, and in a flash he was sitting on Richthofen's tail, spitting a stream of jacketed steel at the Red Devil."

foe were so intermingled that it would have been dangerous to fire. The R.E.8's being observation machines, drew off, but the six *Camels*, being fighting scouts, now fought the whole circus. Every onlooker knew that the German air fiend was present. Richthofen's machine, a Fokker *Tripe* (triplane), was painted a fiery red from engine cowling to tail fin. The rest of the circus were painted dazzle colours.

The end came suddenly. One of the *Camels* dived as if hit. Richthofen, thinking it a ruse, followed in a flash, his forward gun spitting fire. Down they came. And some of the Australian gunners below opened fire with machine guns at the red *Fokker*. Both machines shot earthward past another *Camel*, piloted by Captain Roy Brown, a Canadian ace. As they did so, Captain Brown also dived, and in a flash he was sitting on Richthofen's tail, his gun spitting a stream of jacketed steel at the Red Devil.

The first *Camel* pilot upon whom the Red Devil had dived suddenly pancaked and zoomed upward. But Richthofen never came out of his dive. The *Fokker* struck the ground near an Australian machine gun squad, who claim to this day that their fire brought down the ace.

The German ace was hit by several bullets, but the credit of crashing him was finally awarded to Captain Roy Brown. The Aussies still maintain their claim, however.

So died the great German ace.

Next day they wrapped the German colours around his body and buried him in a little French cemetery behind the British lines within sight of the grey old Towers of Amiens Cathedral. They gave him full military honours and his chief mourners were the British airmen with whom he had fought so gallantly.

His predecessor, Immelmann, was crashed by McCubbin behind the German lines. But the British squadron which crashed him, on the day of his funeral, flew over the lines and dropped a wreath on Immelmann's aerodrome.

* * * * *

The German Flying Corps never regained its prestige after the death of Richthofen. The supremacy of the air was gradually wrested from them. And when the bugles sang truce in the following November, although their famous Guards' Squadron was still in being, the air power of Germany dissolved in defeat.

ROWLAND WALKER.

THE DOG-FIGHT.

UNDER POLAR ICE IN A SUBMARINE

IT is a far cry from the sun-blistered and drought-ravaged plains of Australia to the eerie and unknown world beneath the eternal ice of the Arctic.

Yet it was the vivid memory of things he had seen in Australia when he was a young man that, in after life, caused Sir Hubert Wilkins to turn his attention to Polar exploration, and to attempt to reach the North Pole in a submarine.

In Australia young Wilkins witnessed the appalling horrors of drought. During months of torturing heat he worked to try to save the lives of thousands of sheep and horses dying pitifully of thirst and starvation. When at last the drought broke, and rain came in a downpour, too late to save the shrivelled crops, he saw men running bareheaded into the deluge, and throwing themselves on their knees in the mud in sheer thankfulness.

These were things that no man could forget. He began to wonder whether there was not some way of foretelling the weather, by which these sufferings could be lessened. He studied the problem, and learned how the polar ice caps influenced the weather of the entire earth. It was calculated that the mass of air in the Northern hemisphere in January was ten billion tons greater than in July. This tremendous shifting of air from one half of the globe to the other was attributed to the behaviour of winds at the Poles.

Sir Hubert Wilkins realised that a careful, scientific examination of weather conditions at the Poles would help in forecasting weather all over the world. He made several expeditions to the Arctic and Antarctic, using aeroplanes for flying over the ice.

Then, one day, he met Simon Lake.

Lake was the man who made the first successful ocean voyage in a submerged boat. In 1898 he had travelled from Norfolk, Virginia, to New York in his submarine, the *Argonaut*. Lake offered Sir Hubert Wilkins a new and startling idea.

" Why not go to the North Pole in a submarine ? " he asked.

The idea fired Wilkins' imagination. Here was a new world waiting to be explored. A world that no man had ever entered before, the ice-cold regions beneath the polar oceans.

Lake designed a special submarine for the work. Wilkins set

himself the task of organising a party, and the Wilkins-Ellsworth Trans-arctic Submarine Expedition came into being.

The scheme was to travel over the top of the world from Spitzbergen, by way of the North Pole, to Alaska, a distance of 3,000 miles under the ice.

A submarine, the O-12, was obtained from the United States government, and was remodelled to Simon Lake's designs. The

"They decided to take the chance and go down."

conning-tower was designed like a telescope so that it could be withdrawn into the submarine while the vessel was under the ice. The conning-tower was fitted with an ice-drill, so that holes could be cut in the ice to allow the submarine to come up for air.

The intention was that the submarine should move along the underside of the ice, like a fly walking on a ceiling. For this purpose the top deck was fitted with steel runners like sledge skids, and, in order to prevent the vessel crashing into an unexpected ice barrier, it had a long, flexible arm sticking out in front of the bow, resembling the feelers of an insect.

The submarine was fitted out in a shipyard at Camden, New Jersey, and crossed the Atlantic in the early summer of 1931 to obtain scientific equipment for studying the underwater life of the Arctic. Included in this equipment was a strange device like a mechanical fish, with a long body and a gill-like mouth. As the submarine moved along, water would gush through the mouth, to be filtered through an endless band of muslin. A multitude of varieties of animal and vegetable life would be caught on the muslin, which could be rolled into a spool and preserved for examination later. Before starting on its journey, the O-12 was renamed the *Nautilus*.

On the way to Norway the submarine developed engine trouble, and had to be towed to Tromsoe for repairs. This was an unhappy beginning, but worse troubles were on the way. From Tromsoe the submarine went on to Spitzbergen. This was to be the starting point for the underseas dash beneath the Pole to Alaska.

Once more came trouble. While travelling through the ice floes on the surface, the diving rudders became damaged. It was impossible to repair them. Sir Hubert Wilkins and Captain Sloan Danenhower were faced with a difficult decision. They had to choose between abandoning their trip for the season and going down under the ice with a vessel that might be dangerously difficult to handle.

They decided to take the chance and go down. Captain Sloan Danenhower stood in the conning-tower and surveyed the seascape. The water was thickly sprinkled with cakes of ice of every imaginable shape and size.

" Flood the main ballast ! " ordered the captain.

The submarine went down by the bow. As the vessel slid down into the depths, chunks of ice hammered and grated against the submarine's steel frame. The hollow body of the vessel acted like a sound box, amplifying each bump and crash, so that to her awed passengers it sounded as if the submarine was being smashed to pieces.

Down they went into a strange new world. Through the observation windows they could see glittering fangs of ice, and strange caverns from which darted shoals of fish that dashed and fluttered round the intruder. Fantastic jellyfish floated by. Strange little creatures that looked more like insects than inhabitants of the sea came close to the windows, and then sprang away with active jerks.

But this first dive was experimental. The captain did not wish to go too deep, or too far under the ice until he had satisfied himself that the submarine could be navigated beneath the surface.

He gave the order, " Full astern."

It was a breathless moment. The passengers, with a ceiling of ice above them, gazed anxiously out at the water. Then the fantastic underseas scenery began to glide backwards. The submarine was slowly backing out. It gathered speed, drew clear, and rose to the surface.

The first dive had been made. The passengers in the *Nautilus* had successfully braved dangers such as had been faced by no other living men. The damaged diving rudders, although they did not completely cripple the ship, handicapped it sufficiently for Wilkins to decide that his original intention of a voyage to Alaska was now impossible. He decided to do as much as he could, carrying out investigations into the formation of the sea-bed, the thickness of the ice, the currents and so on, and to gather as many specimens as he possibly could.

But a cruel fate had not finished with the *Nautilus.*

One day there was a rending crash that shook the vessel like a great gale. The ice-drill had shattered itself against the ceiling of ice. This was a serious calamity for, in case of an emergency, the drill offered the only means of escape. If the *Nautilus* had become jammed or disabled, the ice-drill would have been used to cut a hole through the ice, into which the telescopic conning-tower could have been opened so that the crew could escape. Now that safeguard had gone.

The *Nautilus* carried on for a week, during which the crew passed through an arduous time. Frozen water-pipes and clogged oil-feeds caused by the cold, kept the engineers busily engaged thawing out the apparatus. When the vessel came to the surface, where the air was colder than the water under the ice, the moisture in the atmosphere inside the submarine would crystallise into ice on the floors and walls. On submerging again, the ice melted. Everyone's clothing became clammy and there were pools of water on the floor.

Then another unforseen trouble arose. The rush of water caused by the churning of the propellers sucked huge lumps of ice into the steel blades. From time to time a great shudder would run through the vessel as these ice blocks fouled the propellers and gouged pieces out of the blades. One blade was actually bent double.

Although everything possible was done to guard against accidents, the submarine was defeated in its battle with the polar ice. No such voyage had ever been attempted before, therefore it was impossible for the explorers to foresee the perils which they would have to face. They had no experience to go upon, and were forced to learn painfully and expensively from their own mistakes.

At last with the submarine battered and crippled, with two holes in the hull where icy fangs had ripped her, the pioneers retreated to Spitzbergen. Although they had made many valuable scientific discoveries, they were bitterly disappointed, for their main purpose had eluded them.

When a detailed examination of the *Nautilus* was made, it was seen that the damage was too extensive to be repaired. It could not have made the return journey across the Atlantic to America, and so it was scuttled in the North Sea.

STUART CHESMORE.

A giant Iceberg.

A BOY IN THE FOREIGN LEGION

THE hot African sun poured down like molten fire on the rock-strewn, blistered waste surrounding the Algerian town of Perrigaux.

A fierce, warlike band of Arabs had attacked the town. So the authorities sent for the French Foreign Legion to drive the raiders back to the mountains. The 3rd Battalion of the First Regiment, which had its headquarters at Sidi Bel Abbes, was entrained for Perrigaux with orders to disperse the raiders. The Arabs retired to the shelter of the rocks. A trench was dug, and manned by the Legionnaires.

Hard-bitten veterans, raw recruits, and adventurous rascals of all types were to be found in this picturesque band of fighters. But the most remarkable soldier of them all was an English boy, only fifteen years old. His name was A. R. Cooper. Ever since he had first begun to toddle he had been a daring youngster, with a bent for getting into any mischief that offered. Seeking greater thrills, he had decided to run away and join the Legion.

He was a big boy for his age, and looked older than his years. He told the Legion recruiting officer that he was twenty-one. Whether the officer believed him or not, he was accepted as a recruit, enlisting under the name of Cornelius Jean de Bruin, and became Legionnaire 17,692.

The skirmish at Perrigaux was to be his first experience of warfare. He crouched in the trench with his heart thumping against his ribs, while the sun steadily scorched the back of his neck to a brick-red. True, he had been issued with a piece of white linen, intended to be worn on the back of his *kepi* as a covering for his neck, but he had already learned that the Legionnaires did not wear this piece of equipment. They used it to strain their ration of muddy water, in order to make it drinkable!

With his eyes screwed up against the glare of the sun young Cooper watched for some sign of the enemy. He was armed with a very heavy rifle that fired huge bullets, and of a type which had first come into use in 1870, more than forty years earlier. He thought he saw the swirl of a burnous behind a rock. He pulled his trigger. The rifle went off with a deafening racket. The recoil caused the heavy weapon to kick back with such force that the lad was almost knocked off his feet, and left him with a bruised shoulder that was stiff and sore for days afterwards. He fumbled with the bolt to work the ejector, but he was such a beginner at the job that the empty cartridge case stuck, and he had to poke it out with a pencil. A good-natured veteran who was next to him exploded with laughter, and gave him some advice on how to use his rifle.

An hour passed, during which nothing much happened. All along the trench rifles crackled at intervals, but without doing much damage to the Arabs hidden behind the rocks.

"A fierce, warlike band of Arabs had attacked the town."

At last the order was given for the Legionnaires to fix bayonets and charge. Young Cooper went over the top with the rest. In the excitement of the moment he had no time to think about being afraid.

The Legionnaires advanced at a crouching run, stumbling over the rough ground, dodging from cover to cover to avoid the bullets of the Arabs. The Arabs had no fancy for tasting the cold steel of Legion bayonets, and began to retreat. Soon the Legionnaires became widely scattered. Young Cooper found himself running alone. All the Arabs seemed to have scattered into the mountains. Cooper suddenly realised that he was out of breath, footsore from struggling over the hard ground, his muscles aching from the weight of his rifle and heavy kit. He picked a comfortable spot between the rocks, and sat down for a rest.

He had been sitting there for some minutes when an uncanny feeling crept over him. He realised that he was being watched. He jumped to his feet, and discovered that he was surrounded by a band of Arabs who had crept upon him. It was useless to attempt to fight. He was hopelessly outnumbered. The Arabs seized him, took away all his cartridges and other possessions, and talked excitedly among themselves.

At first they did not seem very hostile. But something in the expressions on their faces, and in their gestures, filled young Cooper with fright. One of the Arabs began to prod him, and feel his muscles. Cooper realised that they were planning to take him back to their camp, and torture him. He tore himself away, and snatched up his rifle. Grasping it by the barrel he smashed the butt down on the head of the man who had prodded him, and knocked him down like a ninepin. With screams of rage the whole mob threw themselves on him, knocked him semi-conscious, and dragged him away to their camp. Cooper was flung into a tent. Escape seemed impossible. It appeared that he was doomed to die at the hands of his bloodthirsty captors.

The boy forced himself to keep cool, and tried his hardest to think of a plan to outwit the Arabs. After racking his brains for some time, he had an inspiration. When some of the Arabs came into the tent, he began to chuckle, then to laugh out loud. The Arabs halted and stared at him. Cooper began to creep forward, gazing intently at a fixed spot on the wall of the tent. He made a swift grab, as if trying to catch an invisible fly. Then he turned round and grinned at the Arabs. He held up his thumb, gazed at it and pretended to catch hold of it. Just as his fingers were closing round it he snatched his thumb away, and laughed.

The Arabs looked at each other in vague alarm. Cooper kept up this strange performance, and his captors grew more and more frightened. He moved towards them. They backed hastily out of his reach.

The Arabs thought that Young Cooper was possessed by some evil spirit out of the desert. They were superstitious men, and they feared that it would be unlucky to kill him. After a whispered discussion they withdrew. The lad was left alone. Hours passed. Evening came, and the darkness. Cooper waited in the gloom, shivering with suspense.

"His bluff had worked. They were releasing him."

At last he heard footsteps approaching the tent. The tribal holy man entered, and began to question him about the strength of the attacking forces. Cooper began his imaginary fly-catching again, and replied by giving a fantastic figure that ran into millions. The holy man, speaking in French, asked other questions about the plans and movements of the Legion. To all of these questions Cooper replied with absurd answers. Every moment the lad was afraid that the Arab would lose his temper, and order the captive to be killed.

A sharp command was spoken. Cooper was hustled out of the tent. His heart was in his mouth. What were they going to do

"THE YOUNG LEGIONNAIRE WAS HOPELESSLY OUTNUMBERED."

with him? Did they intend to kill him now? His escort led him outside the camp. Here he expected them to halt, but they did not. They kept marching until they were at a point midway between the camp and the Legion's lines. They halted. They spoke to Cooper in their own language, and pointed. He could have shouted for joy when he realised that they were telling him to go back to Perrigaux. His bluff had worked. They were releasing him.

He began to hurry away. But he had not gone far when he remembered something. The Arabs had taken his rifle from him. Although he had not been in the Legion long, he had already learned that it was a disgrace for a Legionnaire to lose part of his equipment. He hated the idea of going back and admitting to his commanding officer that he had lost his rifle on his very first day of active service. He made up his mind that he would not go back until he had got his own rifle back, or another one in its place.

He crawled among the rocks, and hid himself until the morning. Shortly after dawn he heard the sound of rifle-fire. The Legion was making another attack. Some of the men were passing right by him. He crouched down, hoping that he wouldn't be seen. A bullet from an Arab sniper's rifle droned over his head.

It hit a man a few paces from where Cooper was hiding. The Legionnaire pitched forward on his face, dead. Young Cooper dashed out, snatched up the fallen man's rifle, and charged into the battle.

The Arabs were quelled. Cooper came through the skirmish without a scratch. When it was over, he presented himself to his Captain, as he had been reported missing the night before. He explained exactly what had happened. The Captain chuckled at the story.

"I am very pleased with you, de Bruin," he said. "You will make a good Legionnaire."

The Captain's words came true. At the age of sixteen young Cooper was awarded the Croix de Guerre, the first time this honour had ever been earned by anyone in the Legion.

The Great War was raging, and after fighting with the Legion at the Dardanelles, Cooper was transferred to the British Army. At the end of the War he re-enlisted in the Legion, and served for twelve years, gaining seven medals in the course of a thrilling career. But in spite of the adventures that came afterwards, he never forgot his battle of wits with the Arabs at Perrigaux.

STUART CHESMORE.

FIGHTING AN OIL WELL FIRE

"LOOK out, she's going wild!"

These are words which every oil-field worker dreads to hear. When an oil well goes wild, there is no telling what may happen.

The shout, uttered by a member of a drilling crew at Santa Fé Springs, California, gave the first warning of a grim battle with the forces of nature that was destined to last for a month. Drilling there had resulted in oil being struck in a pocket deep in the earth. The pocket contained gas imprisoned at high pressure, as well as oil. The moment the drill opened up a way to the surface, a mixture of gas and oil gushed upwards at terrific speed. Mixed with the oil was a great deal of sharp grit and sand, which was carried to the surface by the immense pressure. It began to cut through the controlling apparatus which had been erected at the mouth of the well to keep the gusher under control.

The men rushed to close the valves. But they were taken by surprise. Before anything could be done, the well was out of control. It had gone wild. Oil bombarded the sky in a sooty torrent. Instantly the alarm was raised. Sirens, bells, telephones and radio were used to spread the news of the disaster. Police, firemen, guardsmen and ambulance units were mobilised to fight the danger.

A slimy mist began to form in the air, a cloud of oil that spread far and wide, drenching everything, and turning it into a glistening mess. A cordon was formed round the danger area. The roads were closed. Motor cars were turned back. Railway services were curtailed. Aeroplanes were warned by radio to avoid the district. Police toured the houses in the neighbourhood, ordering everyone to extinguish their fires.

The moment that the gusher went wild, everyone was terrified of the greatest danger of all. Fire. A fire might be caused in any one of a hundred ways when the air was saturated with such a highly explosive substance as petrol. It might be caused by the friction of shattered parts of the derrick rubbing together, by the breaking of an electric light bulb while the filament was still hot, by sparks struck from pebbles hurled against the side of the derrick by the roaring gusher, even by the oil itself, rushing through the air at such a fearful speed that the temperature is raised above the danger point. Workmen who toiled with feverish haste to construct a plug to bottle up the well

[Keystone.

An oil gusher.

had their tools wrapped round with cloth for fear of striking a spark that would set fire to the gusher.

The breeze blew the deadly vapour backwards and forwards across the ground. The vapour gathered in pockets and hollows in the ground, a hidden menace to anyone who might blunder in unsuspecting of danger. Search parties were sent out to locate these pockets, and warn the inhabitants of their existence. Vividly in the minds of each one of them was the memory of the terrible occasion at Cushing, in Oklahoma, when petrol vapour from a wild well gathered in a narrow ravine. Two men in a motorcar drove in to it. There was a terrible explosion. The motorcar was blown to pieces, and both men were killed.

Minute by minute conditions grew worse.

Oil was everywhere. Men drew it into their lungs with every breath they took. It drenched their clothes, formed little beads at the end of each eyelash. When they paused for a few moments to refresh themselves with a meal, oil soaked their food, and formed a scum on top of the tea they drank. And all the time, at the back of each man's mind was the dread of the greatest calamity of all, fire.

In spite of all their efforts, the fire came. A flash, a roar, a searing explosion, and the column of gushing oil was transformed into a flaring torch a hundred feet high. Smoke accompanied the flame, smoke in immense volume, rolling down in thick black clouds, choking all who dared to go near it. The heat was intense. The oil-soaked men ran for their lives.

Firemen strove in vain to smother the funnel of flame by deluging it with foam, chemicals and sand. The burning gusher defied them. For days and nights it continued to roar and whistle, spreading a dense pall of sooty smoke far and wide. It was impossible to get near to do anything, on account of the fierce heat.

Then someone had a brilliant idea.

"We can't get at the gusher on the surface," he said. "Why not attack it from underground?"

It was a good suggestion, but it was desperately dangerous. Only men of iron courage could have carried it out. A band of volunteers came forward to see the thing through. Heat-resisting shields were advanced to within sixty feet of the blaze, and behind these a band of heroes worked stubbornly to burrow into the ground. A tunnel, fifteen feet square, was driven down to meet the shaft of the oil well, forty-three feet under the ground. A hole was cut in the casing of the well, and pipes were inserted so that some of the oil could be drawn off, to lessen the pressure.

Then pumps were connected up, and thousands of gallons of mud, water, cement, asbestos and other materials were forced into the well shaft. Bit by bit the shaft became clogged, and the pressure on the gusher grew less. Slowly the tower of flame dwindled in height.

While the tunnellers had been busy trying to bottle up the gusher, engineers had been building a wonderful piece of machinery nicknamed a "Christmas tree." The Christmas tree was a forty-feet long steel pipe, equipped with a series of valves, to be forced into the mouth of the gusher, and plug it.

Twenty-six days after the well had first gone wild, the men decided to make an attempt to cap the gusher. Wind machines were brought into use to blow a gale of air from behind towards the derrick, so as to drive the heat away from them. Hoses sprayed water on

By courtesy of] [*Caterpillar Tractor Co.*

AN OIL WELL ON FIRE.

them as they started forward, dragging the steel plug. The plug was hauled up to the derrick, and swung high over the gusher. It was lowered inch by inch into the dying flame. At last it clamped down over the casing of the well. Men in steel helmets and dripping oilskins threw their weight against levers, forcing them round. Teeth on the mechanical plug gouged out a screw thread on the metal casing of the well, enabling the plug to be screwed tightly into place. Then, as an extra precaution, chains were used to anchor the plug into position.

One at a time the valves were closed. A great shout went up. The gusher had been tamed. The fire was beaten!

The thrilling story of events at Santa Fé is only one of a great many in the romantic history of the oil-fields. When men drill for oil, they are gambling with unknown and titanic forces. Experience has been gained only at the expense of fearful disasters. Even today, the element of risk is almost as great as ever. No two oil pockets are exactly alike. In some, where there is very little gas, the pressure is so low that it is necessary to pump the oil out. In others the force is so terrific that the raging gusher wrecks elaborate and massive machinery before anyone realises what is happening.

On an oil-field in Orange, Texas, when a well was drilled, not oil but mud came hurtling out of the casing. The drilling crew scattered in alarm. Hardly had they got clear when something like an earthquake occurred. The ground opened and the derrick, over a hundred feet in height, sank completely out of sight! When the men gathered their wits and returned to investigate, they found, to their astonishment, that not a sign of their machinery remained. In its place was an almost bottomless pond of water, forty feet in diameter.

On another occasion, at Oklahoma City, a gusher ran wild for three days before it was capped. During that time it coated every building in the city with a film of oil. Every shrub, every flower, every blade of grass in the neighbourhood was sprayed and ruined. Oil covered the streets and had to be left there until dust mixed with it so that it could be washed away. Luckily the gusher itself did not catch fire, but thousands of gallons of oil settled on the surface of a river, and caught alight, setting the water ablaze! The flames floated downstream, and completely destroyed two bridges before the oil burned itself out.

BUILDING A RAILWAY OVER THE SEA

"WE are going to build a railway across the sea!"

This was the startling claim that was made by the pioneers who first visualised the idea of building a railway from Miami to Key West, Florida.

Key West is on a coral island in the Atlantic Ocean, one hundred and fifty miles from the mainland. Everyone was agreed that a railway would be of immense value in speeding up the journey between New York and Cuba. But, of course, you can't lay railway lines across the Atlantic. It is an impossibility.

"It's just a fantastic dream. It couldn't be done," people said.

But there are always pioneers who refuse to believe that anything is impossible. When they hear someone say: "It can't be done," they look upon the words as a challenge.

A party of enthusiastic, imaginative men, surveyed the spot. The difficulties were tremendous. The mainland was a swamp. This swamp, known as the Everglades, was treacherous and primitive. It was overgrown with thick, tropical vegetation. It was infested with swarms of terrible man-eating alligators and with tiny, vicious insects whose poisonous bite meant death.

In this trackless wilderness members of the surveying party wandered off and became lost. Expeditions had to go out to find them. Some of the searches lasted for days, and when the missing men were found again, they were starving, weak with fevers, and on the verge of madness.

Beyond the Everglades was the ocean. Key West was at the end of a long chain of coral islands. Some of the islands were close together. Others were separated by miles of sea. The prospect appeared to be hopeless. But the surveyors refused to be daunted.

"We will drive our railway through the Everglades," they said, "and then we will use the coral islands as stepping stones to carry the track to Key West."

Their enthusiasm conquered the doubts of others. It was decided that where the islands were close together embankments should be built to join them. Where the islands were too far apart they decided to build out embankments from each one until they could go no further, and then to span the distance between the embankments with a viaduct. The viaducts were to be made by building concrete piers on the sea bed. First water-tight cylinders would be lowered into the sea. Then the water would be pumped out, so that men could work inside them, erecting great steel rods to form a framework. Then concrete would be poured into the cylinders, and left for a month to get hard. After a month the outer framework could be removed, leaving a solid concrete pillar on which to lay the girder work of the railway bridge.

There were forty-seven islands in the chain, the distances between them varying from a hundred yards to six miles. Each gap to be filled presented its own problems.

The making of this unique railway is one of the romances of modern engineering. Nearly all the work had to be done from ships and boats. Most of the thousands of workmen lived on the water for months.

All types of craft were brought into service. There were tugs and steamers, motor-boats and launches. Many of the vessels were equipped with cranes, concrete mixers and other machinery. There were fourteen huge houseboats, each with living accommodation for a hundred and forty-four men.

When the workers reached one of the larger islands, they discovered to their amazement that it was inhabited. A man was living there all alone, like a modern Robinson Crusoe. He had lived on the island, undisturbed by any human visitors, for thirty years, feeding on fish and birds which he caught.

For a time work went on smoothly, but tragedy was approaching. The promoters of this gigantic engineering scheme had taken every possible precaution for the workers. All arrangements had been made to keep the industrious army fully supplied with food, medical attention and amusements.

Yet there was one vital factor that had been overlooked. It was the weather. Work was in progress on the Long Key viaduct, which spans over two miles of water, when the weather brought a terrible disaster. In the night the Florida coast was struck by a fearful tornado. With a mighty rushing sound the wind swept down on the half-built railway. An encampment on the mainland was smashed flat. The tornado howled on out to sea. The waves were lashed to mountainous heights. Water smashed against the viaducts with terrible force. Those that had been completed were unhurt by the fury of the storm, but much of the Long Key viaduct was dashed to pieces and carried away.

The men crouched in the houseboats and listened in terror to the booming of the waves, the crash of toppling framework and the

[Keystone.

The first motor car to cross the railway viaduct from Miami to Key West, Florida.

howling of the wind. The boats swung wildly at their anchorages. Thirteen of them managed to ride out the storm, but the fourteenth was swept away. There was panic on the doomed houseboat. Many of the men rushed down into the hold and huddled there in the dark as the tornado carried the craft out into the roaring night.

Among the men who kept their heads was an engineer. He

realised that if the men remained in the hold they would have no chance of saving themselves if the vessel should be wrecked. He went below and urged the men back on deck. Then the houseboat crashed into a reef. It was smashed to pieces almost at once. All the ships in the neighbourhood battled their way through the storm to help in the rescue work. Two ships, one British and the other Italian, lowered their boats on to the wild waters to pick up the victims. Seventy men were saved by these two ships. Other vessels picked up many more.

When the storm abated and daylight came, it was seen that all the uncompleted arches on the Long Key viaduct had been swept away. It was impossible to tell how many lives were lost. Scores of men were missing. But as the days passed, messages began to arrive from ports in various parts of the world, New York, Buenos Ayres, London and Liverpool, reporting that missing men were still alive. After being rescued they had been compelled to remain to the end of the voyage on board the vessels which had saved them.

After this black tragedy, order was restored and work resumed. The railway was completed in 1912. It had cost £32,000 a mile to build. Enormous quantities of materials had been employed. More than a quarter of a million barrels of cement were used. The weight of steel rods used in building the viaducts was 5,700 tons, and it was estimated that the amount of crushed rock used would have been sufficient to make a road a hundred miles long, a yard wide and a yard thick, while sand, if laid in a strip a yard wide and a yard deep, would have stretched for sixty miles. The longest viaduct, known as Knight's Key, is seven miles long. It rests on 185 concrete pillars, and is regarded as one of the greatest railway engineering feats in the world.

Although only three thousand men were at work on the job at any given time, the work was so hazardous and so exhausting that very few men went through the whole job from start to finish, and all together twenty thousand men laboured to build the railway.

As a result of their toil the United States gained a direct railway link with Cuba, for a train ferry operated from Key West to the island, making it possible for a passenger to board the train in New York and travel across the sea to Havana without leaving his carriage.

STUART CHESMORE.

THE ELEPHANT WHO REFUSED TO BE CAUGHT

FOR a week the vast army of native beaters had been moving steadily through the Indian jungle, driving a herd of wild elephants in front of them.

The drive, which was being led by a British official, was nearing its end. The beaters, who had begun the attack in the form of a wide human crescent, were gradually closing in on their quarry. The two tips of the crescent were drawing in so that the line became more and more of a circle with a narrowing gap at the top.

The elephant herd, led by a huge bull-elephant whose great hind legs were marked with scars, lumbered uneasily on through the jungle. Day by day they came nearer to the trap that had been prepared for them. Had the elephants chosen to turn about, and make a break for freedom, the thin human barrier would have been powerless to stop them. But the suspicious elephants did not realise what was in store for them. They knew only that on three sides of them some hidden, creeping danger hedged them in, while in front of them the way was clear. And so, led by the great male with the scarred legs, they went steadily on towards the lurking ambush ahead.

The trap that awaited them was a huge stockade known as a keddah. The keddah was a tremendously strong enclosure, made of thick tree-trunks forming a mighty square fence. The entrance was guarded by a drop gate, which was swung up into the air on hinges. The moment that the last of the elephants entered the keddah the gate would swing down, making them all captives. From the entrance to the keddah ran a funnel-shaped path, fenced in on either side with a network of tree-trunks. The fencing and the stockade had been completely covered with undergrowth to hide its true nature, and make it look like a part of the natural jungle.

At the end of a week of restless travelling the elephant herd reached a ravine. Soon they were to learn that escape had now become almost impossible, for the far end of the ravine was bottled up by thc keddah. Until now the beaters had kept up their remorseless pursuit in silence. But now that the elephants were actually in the ravine, they suddenly revealed their presence beyond all doubt.

Uproar broke loose on all sides. Rifles were fired in the air. Tom-toms were beaten. Men shouted and yelled. Fires were lit.

Panic spread through the herd. At a shambling run the elephants ploughed through the ravine. To them noise meant danger. They increased their pace. They wanted to escape. They little realised that each step they took was bringing them nearer to certain capture.

Near the entrance to the keddah, at the top of a tall tree trunk, a platform had been built for the British official and his friends. The platform served as an observation post from which the whole keddah-drive could be watched and directed. A herd of tame elephants with their mahouts was close at hand. Once the wild herd was trapped, the tame animals would be driven in among them to calm and subdue them. Among the tame herd were a number of trained fighting elephants, who would deal with any of the captives who resisted.

The watching official saw the herd enter the ravine. They came nearer and nearer, approaching the funnel-shaped, fenced-in path.

The official uttered an exclamation.

" Hallo! I know that big fellow who is leading the herd. I can tell him by the scars on his legs! This isn't the first time that he's been in a keddah drive. We almost had him last year, but he got away. He kicked a hole in the side of the stockade, and escaped. That's how he got those scars. H'm. We shall have to watch him. He may prove troublesome." It is not often that an elephant shows fight when he is caught. It is rarer still for one to escape.

The herd came on until it reached the spot where the end of the ravine joined the fenced path. Here the elephants halted uncertainly. In spite of the fact that the trap had been so carefully disguised, they seemed to sense the danger. It was the scarred old tusker who got them moving, and led them down the path. Yard by yard the slanting sides of the path grew narrower, so that the elephants were bunched together. Soon the space became so narrow that they could not go more than two abreast.

Once more they halted, trumpeting in alarm.

Again the scarred leader went on ahead.

" By thunder, I believe he remembers what happened last time!" exclaimed the watching official. " Look! He's going to lead them right into the keddah!"

It certainly seemed as if this was right. The huge elephant was walking straight into the stockade. But, just when he was about to pass through the concealed gate, he halted, and whirled round, blocking the way in. The rest of the herd clustered round,

PART OF THE ELEPHANT HERD.

trying to force past him. He refused to budge. He stood there like a rock.

The beaters, crowding down into the ravine, set up a terrific din. By all means in their power they tried to stampede the herd into rushing the guardian of the gate. The elephants were frightened by the noise behind them, baffled by the powerful leader who barred the way. They fought and kicked within the narrow space. Backwards and forwards the mass surged. Time and again, in their panic, they tried to sweep their leader aside. But the elephant was not to be dislodged. All the efforts of the beaters, all the struggles of the herd, failed to break his stubborn defence. He had been caught once, and he did not intend to be caught again. Nor was he going to allow the rest of his herd to walk into the trap.

A number of native beaters sat astride the top of the stockade, waiting to lower the gate when the herd was safely inside. They shouted and hammered, adding to the confusion, trying to stampede the elephants. They leaned out excitedly to watch the struggle. Without warning, one of the beaters uttered a scream. He had leaned out too far. He overbalanced, and fell right into the opening.

All the beaters set up a wild wailing. Their comrade lay sprawled across the gateway, stunned, within a few inches of the stamping feet of the guardian elephant.

The beater was in a terrifying position. At any moment he might be kicked to death, yet the rest of the natives were too bewildered to know what to do.

The British official, from his watch-tower, saw the whole incident and decided at once to go to the rescue of the native. Swiftly he clambered down the tree-trunk, and scrambled into the stockade. He sprinted towards the gateway, where the whole scene was almost completely blotted out by the fog of choking dust stirred up by the warring elephants.

The ground trembled underfoot. The walls of the stockade quivered as the enraged elephants crashed against the gateway. The noise of stamping and trumpeting was deafening.

More than once, in his dash across the stockade, the British official thought that he would be too late. Time and again a massive foot came within an inch of crushing the limp figure on the ground.

He advanced at a crouching run. The guardian elephant made an impatient rush at the herd, trying to drive them back. This was

"Day by day they came nearer to the trap that had been prepared for them."

the Britisher's chance. He hurled himself forward, caught hold of the native, and dragged him back.

The herd rushed again. The scarred tusker retreated a few yards, passing right over the spot where the beater had been sprawled but a moment before. The heroic official had effected a rescue in the nick of time.

The terrific struggle between the panic-stricken herd and its clever leader lasted for hours.

Night came, and the heroic elephant remained unbeaten. With darkness he changed his tactics. Butting with his head, snorting, trumpeting, he drove the herd back. Then, when he had got them moving in the direction he wanted, he thrust his way to the front, and led them to freedom in a wild stampede.

The beaters were powerless to stop the onrush. It took them all their time to scatter out of the path of the plunging elephants and save themselves from being trampled underfoot. The fence was knocked to pieces. The jungle was stamped flat. The scarred tusker had outwitted his human foes, and saved his herd. Months of arduous work were completely set at nought by the cunning of the big elephant who was too clever to be caught a second time.

STUART CHESMORE.

THE RANGE FEUD

"WHERE have you been, boy? Don't try to lie to me. Have you been out to the J.P. spread again?"

The old man spoke the words bitterly as he eyed his grandson, a wiry sixteen-year-old lad, who had just ridden up to the ranch house.

"I haven't been to the J.P.," declared the boy. "I haven't been off our own range all day."

His grandfather refused to be satisfied.

"You're keeping something back, boy. That horse of yours has been ridden hard. You'd better let me have the truth of it," he insisted.

"'That horse of yours has been hard ridden.'"

"I helped them bring in their new herd of longhorns, across our own range," said the boy. "I figured it was a good idea. I was able to keep an eye on things, and see that they didn't trample our fences."

The grandfather refused to listen to his explanation.

"You stay away from that outfit," he thundered. "They're the biggest bunch of crooks in Kansas. Any flesh-and-blood of mine that so much as speaks to a J.P. cowboy is a traitor to his family."

The vast holdings of the J.P. ranch reached as far as the eastern boundary of the grandfather's holdings. In spite of the efforts of the J.P. cowboys, the cattle frequently broke through the fences, doing damage to the crops and spoiling the springs, and the old man was convinced that the damage was being done on purpose. Although the boy tried to make excuses for their neighbours, his grandfather was too embittered to listen to him.

"THE GROUND SHOOK UNDER THE STAMPING HOOVES OF THE CATTLE. THE AIR WAS THICK WITH DUST."

"'I haven't been to the J.P.,' declared the boy."

"As a matter of fact," said the boy, "the J.P. manager offered to-day for me to work for him."

The old man was aghast.

"You wouldn't work for those scoundrels!" he cried. "If you do, I'll never speak to you again!"

"You don't understand," protested the boy. "What he wants me to do is to watch his new herd from our side of the fence. He's scared that they may make a break, and try to get back to Colorado, where their old range is. The J.P. hasn't got enough men to watch the fence line all the time. Why shouldn't I take the job? It's to our advantage."

But his grandfather refused to listen. He had made up his mind that he hated his neighbours, and nothing would move him. The boy, realising that arguing with his grandfather was like beating at a stone wall, entered the ranch house to get himself a meal. Overhead the sky looked angry. A thunderstorm was threatening. It was the kind of weather to make animals restless. At a time like this, unless the cattle were watched, they might stampede.

The boy came out on to the porch, and looked anxiously towards the south-east, in the direction of the J.P. spread. Abruptly, he caught his breath. A great column of dust was billowing up over the brow of the range. It was coming steadily nearer, moving in as if to meet the storm. There could be only one reason for that cloud of dust. It marked the approach of a herd of stampeding cattle.

"Grandfather!" shouted the boy. "It's the J.P. longhorns. They're heading this way!"

He leaped from the verandah and raced for his horse with giant strides. In one movement he grasped the reins and flung himself into the saddle. Before his grandfather had time to realise what was happening, the boy was galloping in the direction of the stampede. His horse's hooves beat a tattoo of thunder on the hard ground as he clattered at breakneck speed in the direction of the boundary fence. But long before he could get there, the bawling cattle struck the fence, and mowed it down for a space of half a mile. The herd surged forward. Nothing could stop them. The fence stakes were uprooted and snapped like matchsticks. The wire broke like strands of cotton.

"The ground shook under the stamping hooves of the cattle. The air was thick with dust."

The old man watched from the verandah as his grandson galloped furiously towards the onrushing herd. He watched lad and horse dwindle smaller and smaller as they swept down the trail in a cloud of dust.

"The boy's mad. He'll never be able to

do anything. He'll get killed!" cried the old man in agony.

Galloping at a furious speed for over a mile, the boy met the herd at an angle, and bored in towards the leaders. He wanted to head them off, turn them, drive them back in the hope that the rest of the blundering cattle would follow.

The ground shook under the stamping hooves of the cattle. The air was thick with dust. Above the bawling and roaring of the longhorns came the rumble and quaking of the approaching thunderstorm.

Lightning bit through the sky as if to tear the rolling black clouds apart. The first few drops of rain, warm and heavy, pattered on the boy's stetson. It was then that he saw that the stampeding herd was tearing straight towards a group of his grandfather's cattle. In a few moments they would clash. The boy would be nipped between two warring herds.

"His horse's hooves beat a tattoo of thunder on the hard ground."

Already the home cattle were milling round, stirring up the dust, and bellowing. One great bull, who was called Old Hippo, pawed at the ground in defiance, and tossed his great head in fury.

Old Hippo did not wait to be attacked. He rushed in with his head down, making straight for the leader of the J.P. stock. The pair met with a head-on impact, like a pair of runaway locomotives colliding.

Grandfather had got his horse now, and was spurring towards the scene. But he knew that he would be too late. It seemed as if nothing could save the boy. At that moment the skies seemed to burst open. The storm broke with terrific fury. A howling gale, accompanied by great sheets of rain and a terrific bombardment of huge hailstones, came to the rescue at exactly the right moment.

It seemed like a miracle.

The stampeding cattle stopped as abruptly as if they had come face to face with an invisible wall of rock. The smashing deluge of rain, and the mighty bombardment of hail halted them in their tracks. They gathered into a huddled crowd, completely cowed by the fury of the storm, and remained where they were until the fury of it was over. When the deluge ceased, they were completely subdued, and it was no trouble for the boy to turn the herd and drive it back on to the J.P. pastures.

The next day the manager of the J.P. ranch rode over to see the grandfather. He knew that he was risking trouble in doing so, but he felt that he had to come.

"I want to thank the boy for what he did," he said. "It was mighty plucky of him. I'm here to promise that we'll have that fence mended, and put all to rights. Why should we spend all our time quarrelling? Can't we get together, and help each other more?"

The old man looked at him with a strange expression in his eyes. The miracle that he had seen had changed his outlook. He held out his hand.

"Sure, I agree," he said. "I'm mighty proud to shake hands with a friend of the boy's."

STUART CHESMORE.

[Fox Photos.

THE SPIRIT OF ST. LOUIS.
The monoplane in which Colonel Lindbergh made his famous flight all alone across the Atlantic.

"THE FLYING FOOL"

The Transatlantic Flight of Colonel Charles A. Lindbergh.

WHEN, in 1919, two British airmen, John Alcock and Whitten Brown, startled the world by making the first non-stop flight across the North Atlantic, an American sportsman named Raymond Orteig promptly offered a prize of £5,000 to the first man to make a non-stop flight from New York to Paris.

It was a tempting lure for an impossible achievement. Alcock and Brown had flown from Newfoundland to the south of Ireland, a distance of some 1,900 miles, but to fly from New York to Paris involved a journey of nearly double that distance—3,600 miles. There was no aeroplane then in existence capable of carrying enough petrol for so long a flight and it was not, in fact, until seven years later, in 1926, that the design of aircraft had progressed sufficiently for the ambitious venture to be attempted with any hope of success.

The first two attempts, made by French pilots, both ended in disaster, but the hazardous flight seemed to have a peculiar fascination for daring men, and a few months later two famous American airmen,

Commander Richard E. Byrd and Clarence Chamberlain were engaged in a desperate race to complete their preparations and be the first away on a non-stop dash to Paris.

There was also a third competitor, but no one regarded him very seriously. His friends called him "Slim," for he was a tall and slender young man with an unruly mop of fair hair, but the newspapers, when they learned that he was planning to fly the Atlantic alone and in a single-engined aeroplane, dubbed him "The Flying Fool" and prophesied a short life for him. His real name was Charles Augustus Lindbergh and he was very far from being the crazy adventurer that people thought him.

Despite his youth, he had already a record of five years' flying experience behind him, experience that had included a year as a cadet in the U. S. Army Air Service and a long period as chief pilot on the difficult night air-mail service between St. Louis and Chicago. Danger, too, he had known and four times he had saved his life by parachute jumps from doomed machines—a record which no other pilot in the world can equal even to this day.

And so, while all the attention of the public was centred on his more famous rivals, Lindbergh quietly set to work preparing for his great adventure. Every detail of his plans had been carefully thought out, every danger foreseen and every risk considered. While Byrd was planning to use a large, three-engined machine, Lindbergh chose a small single-engined craft because it was more efficient and had a longer range than any multi-engined type. Byrd and Chamberlain were each taking companions to act as navigators and wireless operators. Lindbergh preferred to fly alone and to replace the weight thus saved by an extra amount of fuel which would increase his flying radius by several hundreds of miles. He argued that it was no use having a navigator to tell you how far you were from land if you hadn't enough petrol left to get you there.

The machine he chose for his daring flight was a Ryan monoplane, a small cabin 'plane fitted with a 225 h.p. Wright "Whirlwind" engine and a single wing 47 feet in length. It was a sturdy little machine, but it had one serious defect : the extra petrol tanks necessary for the long range so blocked the pilot's forward view that he could see ahead only by looking out of a side window or by pushing a small periscope up through a hole in the roof. For ordinary flying it would have been a highly dangerous situation, fraught with grave risk of collision in mid-air—but, as Lindbergh explained, he did not anticipate much air traffic in mid-Atlantic!

Lindbergh began his historic flight at San Diego on the Pacific coast of North America and flew right across the American continent to New York, a distance of 2,760 miles. He made only one stop on the way, at St. Louis, where the group of business men who were backing his flight had gathered to wish him luck and to christen his 'plane "The Spirit of St. Louis."

[*Topical* (*L.E.A.*).

Colonel Lindbergh.

For a week Lindbergh waited at New York for a favourable weather report, chafing impatiently at the delay but quite unperturbed by the taunts of the newspapers, who were not slow to suggest that "The Flying Fool" now had "cold feet."

Then, on the evening of May the 19th, 1927, came a report that showed fog over Newfoundland and storms in Europe but reasonably good weather and a following wind over the rest of the route. Lindbergh decided to start at dawn.

There were so many last-minute details to be attended to that he got no rest at all that night and as dawn broke on the morning of May the 20th, he was out on the aerodrome supervising the fuelling of his machine. At last all was ready. Lindbergh took his seat, the cabin door was closed and promptly at 8 o'clock "The Spirit of St.

Louis" roared off the ground and headed out and away on her 3,600 miles non-stop flight to Paris. On the rain-swept aerodrome only a small group of spectators watched the start of a flight that was to make history.

Lindbergh's course, following a Great Circle route, led him northward from New York and during the day he flew over the Bay of Fundy and up the bleak Nova Scotian coast until he sighted Newfoundland. Here he altered course and, as evening fell, steered out into the heart of the Atlantic.

For a while he flew on into the gathering darkness and then, with but little warning, he struck that most dreaded enemy of the airman—fog! At first he attempted to climb above the towering banks into the starlit sky above, but even at 10,000 feet the fog was still thick about him and worse still, a thin film of ice was beginning to form on his wings in the moist and bitterly cold air of those great heights. A coating of ice on his already heavily-overloaded 'plane would mean certain disaster and hurriedly Lindbergh plunged down through the fog to the warmer air of the lower levels. For two hours he flew blindly through the fog, guided only by the dim-lit instruments in his cockpit, until at last there came a rift in the clouds and a welcome glimpse of the risen moon.

All through the night Lindbergh sped on, alone and unseen, above a tumbling waste of dark waters and when at last the dawn broke he celebrated it with a hurried meal of sandwiches and hot

By courtesy of] ["*Flight*"

Colonel Lindbergh landed near Paris, at 10.30 p.m.—33½ hours after leaving New York.

coffee. With the coming of daylight it was now possible for him to discover the effect the wind had been having on his course and, diving down to within a hundred feet of the water, he flew along, gauging the strength and direction of the wind from the breaking crests of the waves beneath him.

Very soon, though, he ran into fog again and to avoid the risk of hitting the water he was forced to ascend again and grope his way blindly through the clouds. Throughout the day the fog persisted in patches and though at every opportunity Lindbergh dived down to fly low above the ocean and check the wind direction, for the greater part of the time he was flying " blind " in the clammy denseness of impenetrable fog-banks.

Then suddenly, in a brief lifting of the fog, he sighted his first ship, a small fishing-boat ; then, further south several more—sure proof that land was near. Joyfully he dived upon the nearest boat, throttled back his engine and circled low above its deck. His intention was to shout and ask the crew to point out the direction of the nearest land but as he came closer and saw no sign of life on board he abandoned the idea, opened up his engine and flew on.

An hour later he sighted land ahead and soon recognised it as the Irish coast. As he drew closer he saw to his delight that he had actually made a landfall within five miles of the point at which he had been aiming—a remarkable achievement after a 1,900 miles' oversea flight in fog and darkness.

It was late afternoon when Lindbergh reached the Irish coast and only 600 miles lay between him and his goal—Paris. Happy and confident now, he sped across the Irish Sea to England, was sighted by a British submarine off Land's End, and at 8.30 p.m., just as the sun was sinking, he was setting out across the Channel bound for the French coast. Guided by the airway beacons along the route he made fast time to Paris and soon after 10 p.m. he was circling in triumph round the Eiffel Tower.

He landed at 10.30 p.m.—33½ hours after leaving New York. He had flown 3,600 miles non-stop at an average speed of 108 miles an hour, the first man to fly from New York to Paris and the first to venture alone upon the hazardous Atlantic crossing.

" The Flying Fool " had become a hero of the world and the idol of a nation.

T. Stanhope Sprigg.

FOUR BELLS IN THE AFTERNOON WATCH

The Sinking of the "LUSITANIA."

IT was four bells in the afternoon watch on the 7th of May, 1915, when the ocean greyhound, *R. M. S. Lusitania*, homeward bound from New York, met her last, great adventure. They were the last bells ever to be struck by human hands on the deck of this famous ship.

The Great War was in progress. Germany, foiled in her attempt to take Paris and capture the Channel ports, had become desperate. The bitter submarine campaign had now begun. Unarmed merchantmen were to be sunk at sight. This had been Germany's challenge a few days before. But no one seriously believed that a civilized nation would in reality outlaw itself by such a violent breach of international law.

Just off the Old Head of Kinsale on the South Irish coast, however, where the seagulls meet the homecoming ships, at 2 p.m. on this fatal day, the incredible thing happened. Captain Turner had reduced the *Lusitania's* speed from twenty to eighteen knots. This had been done so that he might find sufficient water at the Mersey Bar to enable him to sail directly up-stream to Liverpool without stopping to take a pilot aboard. It was known that German submarines had been sighted off the Mersey Bar.

The sea was calm but there was a little haze. That was why the enemy submarine was only briefly glimpsed. The whole thing happened very suddenly.

" Submarine ! " came a warning cry from the watch.

" Where away ? "

" On the starboard bow, Sir ! "

Before the ship could be manœuvred or zig-zagged, the torpedo had been fired. There was a white streak of foam on the surface, then a shadow like a shark moved swiftly through the water.

At such close range, with a ship of such length as the *Lusitania*, it was impossible for the enemy to miss his target.

" Swish ! Boom-m-m ! "

A violent explosion followed. Up on the boat-deck it was merely a muffled, drum-like sound. Down in the engine-room, the din must have been fearful. The starboard side of the huge liner was ripped below the water-line. The *Lusitania* trembled from stem to stern. Instantly volumes of water poured into her holds and engine-room. And the ship began to list heavily to starboard.

" The sea was calm but there was a little haze."

There were 1,253 passengers aboard, including many Americans. There was also a crew of 666. But an eye-witness has told us there was no panic.

" Boat stations ! " was immediately sounded. Then the order was given : " Women and children first ! "

The ship's officers and boat crews hurried off to their stations. Women and children were helped on with their life-jackets, then placed in the boats. These had already been swung out on the davits on reaching the danger zone. The first boats got away. Husbands and fathers shouted a cheery good-bye to wives and children.

"She won't sink! It's just a matter of precaution! We'll meet you at Liverpool!" they shouted.

Even the ship's officers believed the huge liner wouldn't sink. Her water-tight compartments would save her from the fate of the *Titanic*. They were all mistaken. There were only a few minutes left. The *Lusitania* had been too badly holed. She was already preparing to take her last dive.

The officers and crew aboard still carried on. The wireless officer was jazzing the ether with his staccato: '*Zip-zip-zip! Zeep-zeep-zeep! Zip-zip-zip!*' calling up warships, patrols and liners anywhere within hail. On the top deck the rafts were being cast loose. Down below the black squad (stokers and engineers), who had not been killed by the explosion, or scalded to death by the escaping steam, having had no order to abandon ship, kept the tradition of the sea.

"'Submarine!' came a warning cry from the watch."

But the end was very near. The list of the *Lusitania* became suddenly worse. She now hung so far over to starboard that it was impossible to launch the boats on the port side. There followed a rush to the starboard side. But here, even if there had been time, there was not enough room for the whole 1,900 odd passengers and crew.

It was at this moment of time that deeds of heroism, most of which can never be fully recorded, took place. Many children had become separated from their parents. Some of them were crying bitterly. Men passengers helped, even threw some of the children into the

"The first boats got away."

boats hanging on the davits. Other men gave up their life-jackets to women.

"She's going!" shouted someone. "She's sinking!"

So she was.

She leaned so far to starboard now that one of her huge funnels threatened to fall and engulf one of the boats laden with women and children.

Slowly, slowly the *Lusitania* rolled over until her decks became almost vertical, her lower starboard decks already awash. At this moment, on the bridge, Captain Turner, calm as ever, turned to the helmsman at the wheel beside him: "You can go now!" he said. "Try to save yourself! Good-bye!"

The helmsman saluted and looked his skipper in the face. Then he said: "Good-bye, Cap'n!" A moment later both he and the skipper were struggling in the sea.

"The end was very near."

The *Lusitania* had rolled gently over and sunk. Just twenty minutes had elapsed since the torpedo had been fired. Despite every effort to save life, 1,134 men, women and children had gone down to their death.

One survivor says that as the great ship went down a terrible, wailing cry of agony went up. Then for a few minutes there was a fearful, swirling vortex where the vessel had disappeared. Many were drawn down in it. Few of them reappeared. Yet several officers and men did come up again and had miraculous escapes.

Deeds of great heroism and self-sacrifice were performed, however, even after the *Lusitania* had sunk. Doctor C. E. Foss, a passenger, who had helped women and children into the boats, but refused a place for himself, when the ship was about to sink, climbed up the sloping deck and leapt over the port rail. He landed into the sea close to a propeller, which was still turning slowly, but managed to get clear. Dr. Foss then saw a woman holding her child and struggling in the water. He swam to her, and supported them both until a crowded boat drifted by and which could just make room for them.

" I'm all right," explained the doctor. And, seeing another boat some ninety yards away, he swam toward it. This boat was crowded with women. The water was up to the gunwales, and the women were terrified.

" Bale her out ! " cried Foss.

They had nothing to bale with save their hands, however. But they took his advice. By this time Dr. Foss had seen an oar floating by. Being a good swimmer, he reached it, held it by the middle and kept himself afloat.

There were still hundreds of folk in the water, however. Most of them were kept afloat by their life-jackets, but many of them were exhausted. Dr. Foss pushed his oar towards two women.

" Take hold, one at each end ! " he called to them.

Then he began swimming again, pushing the middle of the oar towards a canvas raft on which a few people were seated waiting for the arrival of the patrols. Reaching it, the two women and Foss were dragged aboard the raft. One of the women seemed already dead. But Foss spent forty minutes using artificial respiration to bring her back to consciousness. Later, when one of the first patrols, a small steamer called the *Indian Empire,* reached the spot, all aboard this raft were rescued.

A young Canadian rancher, Donald Barrow, with his young wife was making his first trip to England. They were thrown into the water together when the *Lusitania* sank. Donald supported his wife for nearly four hours until one of the patrol ships picked them up.

Alas, Mrs. Barrow was dead.

Enraged at the inhumanity of the Germans, on reaching Liverpool, Donald Barrow enlisted in the Royal Flying Corps. For nearly two years we served in the same flying squadron.

There were some 700 survivors. Many of them are still alive to-day. Not a few of them owe their lives to some unknown hero who passed them his life-belt, or gave up his place in the boat. Of all the *Lusitania* heroes, however, I must give the palm to an unknown member of the *Black Squad*, who gave his life on that momentous day, trying to save a child and two women from a watery grave. The only available details were given in a letter home, by an officer of a British patrol boat on duty off the South Irish coast a few days after the sinking of the *Lusitania*. The letter runs as follows:

"We recovered seven more bodies to-day. One was a ship's fireman. He had a baby tucked in his belt, and a woman fastened to each arm. He had met his death trying to save them."

Waiting for assistance to arrive.

C2